Iraqi
Phrasebook

Iraqi
Phrasebook

The Essential Language Guide for Contemporary Iraq

Al-Khalesi

Yasin M. Alkalesi, Ph.D.

McGraw·Hill

New York   Chicago   San Francisco   Lisbon   London   Madrid   Mexico City
Milan   New Delhi   San Juan   Seoul   Singapore   Sydney   Toronto

Library of Congress Cataloging-in-Publication Data

Al-Khalesi, Yasin M.
    Iraqi phrasebook : the essential language guide for contemporary Iraq /
Yasin M. Alkalesi.
        p.   cm.
    ISBN 0-07-143511-5 (pbk.)
    1. Arabic language—Dialects—Iraq.   2. Arabic language—
Conversation and phrase books—English.   I. Title.

PJ6825 . A45   2004
492.7'7'09567—dc22   2003066507

2 3 4 5 6 7 8 9 0   LBM/LBM   3 2 1 0 9 8 7 6 5 4

ISBN 0-07-143511-5

McGraw-Hill books are available at special quantity discounts to use as premiums
and sales promotions, or for use in corporate training programs. For more
information, please write to the Director of Special Sales, Professional Publishing,
McGraw-Hill, Two Penn Plaza, New York, NY 10121-2298. Or contact your local
bookstore.

This book is printed on acid-free paper.

DEC 2 2 2004

To the memory of my mother

Contents

Chapter 3

General Phrases   *43*

Chapter 4

Specialized Phrases   *107*

Chapter 5

English–Iraqi Arabic Dictionary   *145*

Acknowledgments

As this text was being written, Iraq witnessed tremendous political and military turmoil. Therefore, additions to the content of the book were necessary to cover some of the new situations in the quickly changing political environment.

Special thanks go to my friend John Spillman Jones for his patience in reading the first draft of the manuscript. I would like to note here that John's dedication to learning Arabic and to understanding its cultural environment is remarkable. I would like to thank my friends Firas Karim, Saad Irubaye, and Laila Darwish for providing me with some of the drawings in the book. My sincere appreciation goes to my friend Jacob Arback for his advice and help. I am also grateful to the people at McGraw-Hill for their editorial and production work, especially Christopher Brown, Executive Editor, for his assistance and insight.

Finally, to my companion in life, Jytte Paris Springer, I extend special gratitude for her continual encouragement and enthusiasm. And I am forever indebted to my father for creating in our home an environment of learning and knowledge seeking.

Introduction

Arabic is a Semitic language written from right to left. It has two
forms: classical (also known as Modern Standard Arabic [MSA]) and
colloquial. Many other languages also have similar divisions between
formal and informal registers. Modern Standard Arabic is the stan-
dardized language of reading and writing throughout the Arab
world. Colloquial Arabic, the spoken language of everyday activities,
varies from one Arab country to another and has many dialects—
Egyptian Arabic, Moroccan Arabic, Lebanese Arabic, Iraqi Arabic,
and so on. The main differences between these dialects are found in
pronunciation, everyday expressions, and idiomatic phrases.

This book presents the Iraqi dialect of Arabic, and more specifi-
cally, the dialect spoken in and around the capital city of Baghdad. It
is the most widely used and understood form of the language
throughout Iraq.

Iraqi Phrasebook uses a transcription system of phonetic writing
to express the sounds of Iraqi Arabic (see Chapter 1). Arabic script
has been abandoned in favor of phonetics to make this book easy for
the English speaker to use. There is no need to learn a whole new
alphabet in order to speak Iraqi Arabic and start communicating

immediately. Readers are advised to study the phonetic system well to help them learn the pronunciation of Iraqi words.

This text has been designed to provide the words and phrases travelers will need most often during their time in Iraq. The chapters are built around everyday situations. Words and phrases used throughout the chapters are usually given in the masculine singular form. For other variations, such as feminine and plural forms, and the type of verb conjugation, refer to the dictionary in Chapter 5.

In addition to lists of useful words and phrases, much of the language in this book is presented in a conversational format to show you examples of how the phrases fit together and to help you communicate. This also ensures that many of the phrases you'll need in a specific situation can all be found together for easy reference.

Abbreviations

The following list contains the abbreviations used in this book.

adj.	adjective
dl.	dual
dv	double verb
f.	feminine
f.dl.	feminine dual
f.pl.	feminine plural
f.sing.	feminine singular
hv	hollow verb
iv	imperative verb
m.	masculine
m.dl.	masculine dual
m.pl.	masculine plural
m.sing.	masculine singular
n.	noun
pl.	plural
rv	regular verb
sing.	singular
v.	verb
wv	weak verb

Chapter **1**

Introduction to Iraqi Arabic

Iraqi Alphabet and Translation

Iraqi Arabic has thirty-one consonant sounds, almost all of which have equivalents in English and other European languages. The few with no equivalents in other languages will require more practice by learners.

Consonants

It is very important that you familiarize yourself with the phonetic writing (transcription) and the sounds of the consonants that follow. Notice that an underlined letter (such as "t," "z," or "s") has a different sound than "t," "z," and "s." The underline represents the "thick" version of each letter, pronounced with the tip of the tongue on the roof of the mouth rather than against the teeth. Two underlined letters (for example, "dh" or "kh") are read as one sound ("dh" as in "that" and "kh" as in "Bach"). The following table provides a list of the transcriptions used in this book, as well as a pronunciation guide.

Transcription	As in	Example
'	uh-oh	sa'al
9	—	9aali (almost silent *ah*, pronounced deep in the back of the throat)
b	bird	beit
ch	chair	chamcha
d	deed	daff
d͟h	that	d͟haab
f	father	faakir
g	gag	gahwa
g͟h	Parisien	g͟haali
h	hat	hal
h͟	—	h͟aar (voiceless, strongly whispered deep in the throat, similar to the sound produced by someone who just burned his mouth on hot coffee)
j	judge	jaar
k	kilo	kilma
k͟h	Bach, auch	k͟haaf
l	lid	leila
l͟	bell	al͟la (emphatic "l")
m	mom	mahal
n	noon	nahaar

p	pencil	parda
q	—	qaal (like the "c" in "cool" but produced farther back in the throat)
r	Alhambra	nuur
s	sit	sarr
s̱	—	saad (emphatic "s," similar to the "s" in "sum," with the central part of the tongue depressed and the back part slightly raised)
sh	dish	shaaf
t	tight	taam
ṯ	ultra	baṯṯ
th	thin	thaalith
w	well	waalid
y	yellow	yoom
z	zebra	zeit
ẕ	—	zeif (emphatic sound made by pronouncing "z" with the tip of the tongue against the roof of the mouth)

Vowels

Iraqi vowels, like all other Arabic vowels, are of two types, short and long. The timing of the length of Arabic vowels is very important, because a short or a long vowel in the same word gives quite different meanings, as in "jamal" (camel) and "jamaal" (beauty).

Short Vowels

Vowel	As in	Example
a	at	qalam (pencil)
i	fit, give	filfil (pepper)
u	put	ruzz (rice)
o	piano	raadio (radio)

Long Vowels

Vowel	As in	Example
aa	father	jaab (to bring)
ei	wait	beit (house)
ii	feet, beet	tiin (figs)
uu	root, cool	nuur (light)
oo	dog, fog	mooj (waves)

Diphthongs

Diphthongs in Iraqi Arabic are combinations of a short ("a") or long ("aa") vowel and a semivowel ("w" or "y").

Diphthong	As in	Example
aw/aaw	how, cow	mawja (one wave)/kaawli (gypsy)
ay/aay	by, bright	jaysh (army)/jaay (coming)

Word Stress

All Iraqi words have one "stress syllable" that is pronounced more forcefully than the others. A stress syllable is one that contains a long vowel followed by a consonant, as in the word "bar**ii**d," or a short vowel followed by two or more consonants, as in the word "h**uww**a." In words with two or more syllables, the stress is always on the last syllable, as in "ju⁹**aan**/ju⁹aan**iin**/ju⁹aan**aat**." If the word has none of these characteristics, then the stress falls on the beginning of the word, as in the word "**ri**kab."

Grammar

Nouns

Iraqi Arabic nouns are either masculine (*m.*) or feminine (*f.*) in gender. Most feminine words end with the vowel "a," as in "madrasa" (school), and most masculine words end in a consonant, as in "maktab" (office), although there are exceptions. For words that refer to people (animate objects), the gender can be changed by simply adding or omitting the feminine ending -**a**. Inanimate objects, such as an office or school, can only be masculine or feminine.

Masculine	Feminine
ibin (son)	ibna (daughter)
taalib (student)	taaliba (student)
daliil (guide)	daliila (guide)
kalb (dog)	kalba (dog)

Most nouns have three forms: singular (*sing.*), dual (*dl.*), and plural (*pl.*). The most common masculine plural is made by adding the suffix **-iin**, and the dual is made by adding the suffix **-ein**. The feminine plural is most often made by adding the suffix **-aat**, and the feminine dual by adding the suffix **-tein**.

Masculine singular	Masculine dual	Masculine plural
mu⁹allim	mu⁹allmein	mu⁹allimiin
fallaah	fallaahein	fallaahiin
mudarris	mudarrisein	mudarrisiin
muhandis	muhandisein	muhandisiin

Feminine singular	Feminine dual	Feminine plural
sayyaara	sayyaartein	sayyaaraat
taaliba	taalibtein	taalibaat
mu⁹allima	mu⁹allimtein	mu⁹allimaat
fallaaha	fallaahtein	fallaahaat

Adjectives

In Arabic, the adjective follows the noun and agrees with its gender, its number, and whether it is definite or indefinite (explained in the next section). Adjectives have different forms for masculine, feminine, and plural. The masculine adjective usually ends in a consonant (jamiil [beautiful]); the feminine ends with the suffix -**a** (jamiila); and the plural ends in -**iin** (jamiiliin, *m.*) or -**aat** (jamiilaat, *f.*). Another common adjective plural is the "broken plural," as with the word "kabiira" (big): kabiir (*m.*), kabirra (*f.*), kbaar (*m.,f., pl.*).

Masculine Noun-Adjective

Singular	*Plural*	*English*
taalib jdiid	tullaab jdaad	new student/s
aani zein.	ihna zeiniin.	I am/We are well.
taalib juu⁹aan	tullaab ju⁹aaniin	hungry student/s

Feminine Noun-Adjective

Singular	*Plural*	*English*
taaliba jamiila	taalibaat jamiilaat	new student/s
aani zeina.	ihna zeinaat.	I am/We are well.
taaliba juu⁹aana	taalibaat ju⁹aanaat	hungry student/s

The Article "The"

The prefix **il-** added to nouns and adjectives is the equivalent of the English "the." With some words or combinations of words, the vowel "i" in the article may disappear or switch position to make **li-**. If the prefix **il-** is added to a word that begins with the consonants t, t̠, th, j, ch, d, d̠h, r, z, s, sh, s̠, or n, the letter "l" of the article is replaced by the first letter of the word, resulting in double consonants at the beginning of the word.

Indefinite	**Definite**
qalam (a pencil)	il-qalam (the pencil)
mudiir (a director)	il-mudiir (the director)
ktaab (a book)	li-ktaab (the book)
hsaab (a bill)	li-hsaab (the bill)
saa⁹a (a watch)	is-saa⁹a (the watch)
tabiib (a doctor)	it-tabiib (the doctor)

Pronouns

Pronouns are either independent words or suffixes attached to nouns
or verbs. Arabic has no equivalent to the pronoun "it." In Arabic, "it"
is expressed by the pronouns "huwwa" (he), "hiyya" (she), or
"humma" (they), since all nouns are either feminine or masculine.

Independent Pronouns Independent pronouns are personal
pronouns and are always the subject of a statement.

English	**Arabic**
I (*m./f.*)	aani
you (*m.*)	inta
you (*f.*)	inti
he	huwwa
she	hiyya
we (*m./f.*)	ihna
you (*m./f.*)	intu
they (*m./f.*)	humma

Example	Meaning
aani zein.	I (*m.*) am well.
aani zeina.	I (*f.*) am well
inta zein.	You (*m.*) are well.
inti zeina.	You (*f.*) are well.
huwwa zein.	He is well.
hiyya zeina.	She is well.
iḥna zeiniin.	We (*m.pl.*) are well.
iḥna zeinaat.	We (*f.pl.*) are well.
intu zeiniin.	You (*m.pl.*) are well.
intu zeinaat.	You (*f.pl.*) are well.
humma zeiniin.	They (*m.pl.*) are well.
humma zeinaat.	They (*f.pl.*) are well.

Pronoun Suffixes Pronoun suffixes are attached to nouns, verbs, and some other words such as prepositions. A noun plus a pronoun suffix indicates possession (Mary's). A verb plus a pronoun suffix indicates the object of the verb.

With Noun	With Verb	Pronoun
my	me	-i, -ti, -ni
our	us	-na
your (*m.*)	you	-ak
your (*f.*)	you	-ich
your (*pl.*)	you	-kum
his	him	-a
her	her	-ha
their	them	-hum

Note that **-i** and **-ti** are used only with masculine and feminine nouns, respectively, and **-ni** is used only with verbs.

qala**mi**	my pencil
sayyaar**ti**	my car
huwwa yḥib**ni**.	He likes me.

Verbs

Iraqi verbs have two basic tenses: past and present/future. In addition to the two tenses, most verbs have an imperative form. The past tense is formed by adding suffixes to the verb. The present tense is generally formed by adding prefixes to the verb, although sometimes suffixes are also needed. Each verb tense has eight forms corresponding to the independent pronouns (aani, inta, inti, huwwa, hiyya, iḥna, intu, and humma). Each Arabic verb consists of a root—which provides the meaning of the verb—and a prefix, a suffix, or both—which define the doer of the action. There are four main types of roots: regular, double, hollow, and weak. Notice that in the past tense these four roots have different conjugations. The following are model conjugation tables that can be used for reference. An asterisk (*) indicates identical conjugation.

Past Tense

The Regular Verb: diras (he studied)

Pronoun	Suffix	Verb	Meaning
I, aani	-it	dirasit*	I studied
we, iḥna	-na	dirasna	we studied

you (*m.*), inta	-it	dirasit*	you studied
you (*f.*), inti	-ti	dirasti	you studied
you (*pl.*), intu	-tu	dirastu	you studied
he, huwwa	—	diras	he studied
she, hiyya	-at	dirsat	she studied
they, humma	-aw	dirsaw	they studied

The Hollow Verb: saaq (he drove)

Pronoun	Suffix	Verb	Meaning
I, aani	-it	siqit*	I drove
we, iḥna	-na	siqna	we drove
you (*m.*), inta	-it	siqit*	you drove
you (*f.*), inti	-ti	siqti	you drove
you (*pl.*), intu	-tu	siqtu	you drove
he, huwwa	—	saaq	he drove
she, hiyya	-at	saaqat	she drove
they, humma	-aw	saaqaw	they drove

The Double Verb: hatt (he put)

Pronoun	Suffix	Verb	Meaning
I, aani	-eit	hatteit*	I put
we, iḥna	-eina	hatteina	we put
you (*m.*), inta	-eit	hatteit*	you put
you (*f.*), inti	-eiti	hatteiti	you put
you (*pl.*), intu	-eitu	hatteitu	you put
he, huwwa	—	hatt	he put
she, hiyya	-at	hattat	she put
they, humma	-aw	hattaw	they put

The Weak Verb: nisa (he forgot)

Pronoun	Suffix	Verb	Meaning
I, aani	-eit	niseit*	I forgot
we, iḥna	-eina	niseina	we forgot
you (*m.*), inta	-eit	niseit*	you forgot
you (*f.*), inti	-eiti	niseiti	you forgot
you (*pl.*), intu	-eitu	niseitu	you forgot
he, huwwa	—	nisa	he forgot
she, hiyya	-at	nisat	she forgot
they, humma	-aw	nisaw	they forgot

Present Tense   The conjugations of the present tense of the four verb roots are identical.

The Regular Verb: yudrus (he studies)

Pronoun	Prefix/Suffix	Verb	Meaning
I	a-	adrus	I study
we	n/ni/nu	nudrus	we study
you (*m.*)	t/ti/tu	tudrus*	you study
you (*f.*)	t/ti/tu . . . iin	tudursiin	you study
you (*pl.*)	t/ti/tu . . . uun	tudursuun	you study
he	y/yi/yu	yudrus	he studies
she	t/ti/tu	tudrus*	she studies
they	y/yi/yu . . . uun	yudursuun	they study

12

The Future Tense In Iraqi Arabic, there are two ways to form the future tense. Add one of two prefixes, **rah-** or **ha-** (will, shall, going to), to the present tense form.

rah-adrus/ha-drus.	I will study.
rah-nsaafir/ha-nsaafir.	We will travel.

The Prefix da- (-ing) In English, the suffix -ing is used to indicate a progressive action—that is, something that is ongoing or presently occurring. In Iraqi Arabic, the prefix **da-** plus the present tense forms the progressive.

da-yudrus.	He is studying.
da-nsaafir.	We are traveling.
da-ashrab chaay.	I am drinking tea.

Negatives

There are four basic negation words in Iraqi Arabic: "muu" (not), "maa/ma-" (not), "laa/la" (no), and "wala" (nor, not). They precede the words to be negated. "Muu" is used to negate adjectives and adverbs; "maa" is used to negate verbs. "Laa/la" and "wala" are used in different constructions.

aani muu ⁹iraaqi.	I am not an Iraqi.
huwwa muu juu⁹aan.	He is not hungry.
hiyya ma-tsaafir.	She is not traveling.
inta Amriiki?	Are you an American?
laa. (reply)	No.
aani muu ju⁹aan wala ta⁹baan.	I am neither hungry nor tired.

13

Forming Questions

As in English, questions in Iraqi Arabic are formed either by changing the inflection of a sentence or by adding an interrogative word to it. The following are some of the most common interrogative words.

What?   shunu/sh-?
     What is your name?   *shunu ismak?, shi-smak?*
Where?   wein?
     Where is Babylon?   *wein Baabil?*
How much/long/far?   shgadd?
     How long did you study Arabic?   *shgadd dirasat ⁹arabi?*
     How much is one kilo of meat?   *shgadd kilo l-laham?*
When?   shwakit?
     When did you drive the car?   *shwakit siqit is-sayyaara?*
Which?   ay?/yaa?
     Which post office is near?   *ay bariid qariib?*
How much?/What time?   beish?/ibbeish?
     How much is the beer?   *beish il-biira?*
     What time is it?   *ibbeish is-saa⁹a?*
How many?   kam?/cham?
     How many museums in Baghdad?   *kam mathaf ib-Baghdaad?*
How?   shloon?
     How are you?   *shloonak?*
Why?   leish?
     Why are you upset?   *leish za⁹laan?*
Is . . . ?/Are . . . ?   hal?
     Are you (m.) from America?   *hal inta min Amriika?, inta min Amriika?*

Where from?	mnein?
Where did you come from?	*mnein ijeit?*
Who?/Whom?	minu?
Who is she?	*minu hiyya?*
Whose?	maalman?/ilman?
Whose passport is this?	*maalman il-paasport?*

Prepositions

The main prepositions in Iraqi Arabic are listed here for reference. These prepositions may appear by themselves, with attached pronouns, or as prefixes at the beginning of words.

at [someone's] place	9ind
after	ba9ad
before	gabul
behind	wara
between	bein
in, at, by	b-/bi-
in front of	giddaam
inside	jawwa, daakhil
on, upon, about	9ala/9a-
over, above	foog
to, for	l-/li-, ili
under	taht
with	ma9a, wiyya

Conjunctions

Conjunctions are used to connect words, phrases, or clauses.

although	walaw
and	wa/w-
because	li-an
but	laakin, bass
if	loo, idha
or	loo, aw
since	min
so that	hatta
until	hatta, lil

There Is/Are

The invariable word "aku" (there is/are) is an understandably important word in Iraqi Arabic, as it is in any language. It is negated with the prefix **maa-**.

There is a policeman here.	aku shurti hnaa.
No, there is no policeman here.	laa, maaku shurti hnaa.
There are many cars.	aku sayyaaraat hwaaya.
There aren't many cars.	maaku sayyaaraat hwaaya.

This/That

Two groups of demonstrative words in Iraqi Arabic are equivalent to the English demonstratives "this/these" and "that/those." Each group has three forms: masculine, feminine, and plural.

this (*m.*)	haadha
this (*f.*)	haadhi
these (*m./f.*)	hadhoola

that (*m.*)	hadhaak
that (*f.*)	hadhiich
those (*m./f.*)	hadhoolaak

Composing Basic Sentences

There are three basic ways to form statements or sentences in Iraqi Arabic.

Phrases A phrase consists of a noun and an adjective, either with or without a definite article ("the").

hot tea	chaay haar
the hot tea	ich-chaay il-haar
small room	ghurfa zghayra

Statements Statements of the "equational" type normally consist of a subject and a predicate. In English these sentences are formed with the verb "to be."

The tea is hot.	ich-chaay haar.
Traveling is expensive.	is-safar ghaali.
I am Italian.	aani Itaali.
Ahmad is in the office.	Ahmad bil-maktab.

Sentences Sentences have verbs, subjects, and sometimes objects.

I visited Iraq.	zirit il-⁹iraaq.
He works in a big office.	yushtug͟hul b-maktab chibiir.
She drove the car.	saaqat is-sayyaara.
He is thinking.	huwwa yfakkir.

Chapter **2**

Getting Started

Socializing

Arabs generally use elaborate sets of greetings and courteous expressions when meeting one another. There are formal greetings among strangers and informal greetings among friends. Greetings always include an inquiry about the well-being of the members of the other person's family and friends. As in the Western world, it's customary to shake hands when you meet people. When you sit down, you are always greeted with the expression "allaa bil-kheir" (God bless), to which you should reply with the same phrase. Travelers are advised to stick to one of the standard greetings. Certain circumstances require a specific set of words and expressions that should be learned and used appropriately.

Note: Most often, only masculine forms of words and phrases are used throughout this text. For the feminine or plural, see the dictionary in Chapter 5. Multiple translations for the same word are separated with a comma. When the plural is given, the words are separated with a slash (/).

Basic Vocabulary and Expressions

Mr.	sayyid
Mrs.	sayyida
Miss	aanisa
Excuse me.	⁹an idhnak.
Excused. (reply)	tfazzal.
yes (formal)	na⁹am
yes (informal)	'ii
no	laa
OK	maykhaalif
please (requesting something)	min fazlak, rajaa'an
Please. (reply)	tfazzal.
Sorry., Pardon me.	⁹afwan.
God willing (a very common expression)	inshaalla
God willing, I will visit you.	inshalla, azuurak.
Congratulations.	mabruuk.
Thanks. (reply)	shukran.
Hurry up.	yalla.
Hurry up and go.	yalla, ruuh.

Greetings and Everyday Expressions (tahiyyaat)

Hello. (informal)	marhaba.
Hello. (reply)	marhaba.
Hello. (formal)	as-salaamu ⁹laykum. (*lit.* peace be upon you)
Hello. (reply)	wa ⁹alaykumu s-salaam.
How are you (*m.*)?	shloonak?

I am well, praise God.	aani zein, il-ḥamdu li-llaah.
How are you (*m.*)? (reply)	inta shloonak?
Please sit down.	tfazzal istariiḥ.
Thank you.	shukran.
Thank you very much.	shukran jaziilan.
God bless. (idiom, after one sits down)	allaa bil-kheir.
God bless. (reply)	allaa bil-kheir.
What is happening?	shaku maaku?
Nothing. (a reply)	maaku shii.

Timely Greetings (taḥiyyaat yawmiyya)

Good morning.	ṣabaaḥ il-kheir.
Good morning. (reply)	ṣabaaḥ in-nuur.
Good afternoon/evening.	masaa' il-kheir.
Good afternoon. (reply)	masaa' in-nuur.
Good night.	tisbaḥ 9ala kheir.
Good-bye.	ma9a s-salaama., fiimaanillaa.

Small Talk (dardasha)

Hello.	marhaba.
What's your name?	sh-ismak?
My name is . . .	ismi . . .
I am honored.	tsharrafna.
The honor is ours. (reply)	wilna ish-sharaf.
Where are you from?	inta min wein?

I am from Paris.	aani min Paariis.
Canada.	*Kanada.*
I like Canada.	ahibb Kanada.
I'd like to visit Canada.	ahibb azuur Kanada.
What kind of work do you do?	sh-tushtughul?
I am a businessman.	aani rajul a⁹maal.
How long are you staying here?	shgadd rah-tibqa hnaa?
One month.	shahar waahid.
Where are you staying?	wein naazil?
At the Mansour Hotel.	b-Findiq il-Mansuur.
Do you like the hotel?	y⁹ijbak il-findiq?
I like it.	yi⁹jibni.
I don't like it.	ma-yi⁹jibni.
It's very nice.	zein hwaaya.
Would you like to visit me?	thibb tzuurni?
Later, God willing.	ba⁹dein, inshaalla.
Good-bye.	ma⁹a s-salaama.

Meeting People/Introductions
(muqaabala/ta⁹aaruf)

I'd like to introduce my friend,	ahibb a⁹arfak ⁹ala
Mr. Ahmad.	sadiiqii sayyid Ahmad.
my wife, Mrs. Samiera.	*zoojti sayyida Samiira.*
my husband, Mr. Sami.	*zooji sayyid Saami.*
We are honored.	tsharrafna.
The honor is ours. (reply)	wilna ish-sharaf.
How are you?	shloonak?
Well, praise God.	zein, il-hamdu lillaah.

How are you? (reply)	shloonak inta?
Please sit down.	tfazzal istariih.
Thank you.	shukran.
God bless.	allaa bil-kheir.
I am an archaeologist.	aani aathaari.
a businessman.	*rajul a⁹maal.*
a doctor.	*tabiib, diktoor.*
an engineer.	*muhandis.*
a journalist.	*sahafi.*
a Ph.D.	*diktoor, ustaadh.*
a photographer.	*musawwir.*
a scientist.	*⁹aalim.*
a student.	*taalib.*
a teacher.	*mu⁹allim.*
What kind of work do you do?	sh-tushtughul?
Do you like Baghdad?	thibb Baghdaad?
I like it very much.	ahibha hwaaya.
Have you visited Babylon?	zirit Baabil?
No.	laa.
Yes.	na⁹am.
Let's take a picture together.	khalliina naakhudh suura suwa.
Why not?	leish laa?
Smile, all of you.	ibtasmu kulkum.
I'd like to see you again.	ahibb ashuufak marra thaanya.
We can meet tomorrow at the hotel.	mumkin nitlaaga baachir bil-findiq.
Which hotel?	ay findiq?
The Babylon Hotel.	Findiq Baabil.
Where is the hotel?	wein il-findiq?

At what time?	ibbeish is-saa⁹a?
At 7:00 P.M.	is-saa⁹a sab⁹a masaa'an.
OK.	zein.

Saying Good-Bye *(ma'a s-salaama)*

Nice to have met you.	tsharrafna b-ma⁹rifatkum.
The honor was ours.	wilna ish-sharaf.
Thank you very much for your hospitality.	shukran jaziilan ⁹ala ziyaafatkum.
I hope you liked the food, God willing.	inshaalla, ⁹ijabkum il-akil.
It has been a wonderful evening.	kaanat leila jamiila jiddan.
Please say hello to . . .	rajaa'an sallimli ⁹ala . . .
I'd like to have your phone number.	ahibb aakhudh raqam talafoonak.
Here is my number.	tfazzal haadha raqmi.
This is my address.	haadha ⁹unwaani.
What's your address?	shunu ⁹unwaanak?
Please write to me.	rajaa'an, iktibli.
I will send you the pictures.	rah-adizlak is-suwar.
We must go now.	laazim nruuh hissa.
It is still early.	ba⁹ad wakit.
I am busy.	aani mashghuul.
Do you need a ride?	mihtaaj tawsiila?
No, thanks.	laa, shukran.
I have a car.	⁹indi sayyaara.
You must visit us soon.	laazim tzuuruuna qariiban.

Yes, God willing.	na⁹am, inshaalla.
Good-bye.	ma⁹a s-salaama.

Speaking Arabic (il-lugha l-⁹arabiyya)

I don't speak Arabic.	maa atkallam ⁹arabi.
I know only a few words.	a⁹ruf bass kalimaat qaliila.
Do you speak English?	titkallam Ingiliizi?
Arabic?	*⁹arabi?*
Does anyone here speak English?	aku waahid hnaa yitkallam Ingiliizi?
I have a small book with me.	⁹indi ktaab zghyyir.
It has Arabic-English phrases.	bii kalimaat ⁹arabi-Ingiliizi.
Please help me with this word.	rajaa'an saa⁹idni b-haadhi l-kilma.
What does this word mean?	shunu ma⁹na haadhi il-kilma?
I understand.	fihamit.
I don't understand.	ma-fhamit.
Do you understand?	tifham?
What are you saying?	shunu da-tguul?
How do you say . . . in Arabic?	shloon tguul . . . bil-⁹arabi?
Please speak slowly.	rajaa'an tkallam ⁹ala keifak.
Please read this for me.	rajaa'an iqraali haadhi.
Please repeat it.	rajaa'an ⁹iid-ha li.
Please translate this word for me.	rajaa'an tarjumli haadhi l-kilma.
Please write it down for me.	rajaa'an iktibha li.
Arabic is a difficult language.	il-⁹arabi lugha sa⁹ba.
English is an easy language.	il-Ingiliizi lugha sahla.

| You speak good English. | inta titkallam Ingiliizi zein. |
| Thank you. | shukran. |

Visiting a Family (ziyaarat ⁹aa'ila)

Thank you for inviting us to your house.	shukran li-da⁹iwtak ilna l-beitak.
to visit your family.	*l-ziyaarat ⁹aa'iltak.*
This is . . .	haadha (*m.*) or haadhi (*f.*) . . .
my aunt.	*khaalti.*
my brother.	*akhi.*
my daughter.	*binti.*
my father.	*waaldi.*
my friend.	*sadiiqi.*
my grandfather.	*jiddi.*
my grandmother.	*jiddiiti.*
my husband.	*zooji.*
my mother.	*waalidti.*
my sister.	*ukhti*
my son.	*ibni.*
my uncle.	*khaali.*
my wife.	*zoojti.*
Are you (*m.*) married?	inta mizzawwij?
Yes, I am married.	na⁹am, aani mizzawwij.
No, I am not married.	laa, aani ma-mizzawwij.
I am single.	aani a⁹zab.
I am engaged.	aani khaatub.
This is my fiancée.	haadhi khatiibti.
I am divorced.	aani mtallig.

Do you have children?	⁹indak wilid?
Yes, I have a son and a daughter.	na⁹am, ⁹indi walad wi-bnayya.
How old are they?	shgadd ⁹umurhum?
Do your children go to school?	wildak yruuhuun lil-madrasa?
May God keep them for you.	alla ykhalliilak yyaahum.
Praise God, you have a large family.	maashaalla, ⁹aa'iltak chibiira.
Thank you.	shukran.
Where are you staying?	wein naazil?
At a hotel.	b-findiq.
With a friend.	⁹ind sadiiq.
You have honored us with your visit.	sharrafitna bi-zyaartak.
The honor is ours. (reply)	wilna sh-sharaf.
Good-bye.	ma⁹a s-salaama.

Numbers

Basic Words and Phrases

equal	ysaawi
half	nuss
math, account, bill	hsaab
number/s	raqam/arqaam
percent	nisba mi'awiyya
quarter	rubu⁹

Cardinal Numbers

0	sifir
1	waahid (*m.*)/wihda (*f.*)
2	thnein (*m.*)/thintein (*f.*)
3	tlaatha
4	arba^{9}a
5	khamsa
6	sitta
7	sab^{9}a
8	thmaanya
9	tis^{9}a
10	^{9}ashra
11	da^{9}ash
12	thna^{9}ash
13	tlat-ta^{9}ash
14	arba^9-ta^{9}ash
15	khmus-ta^{9}ash
16	sit-ta^{9}ash
17	sbaa-ta^{9}ash
18	thmun-ta^{9}ash
19	tsaa-ta^{9}ash
20	^{9}ishriin

Numbers three through nine can be increased to multiples of ten by adding the suffix **-iin** after dropping the final vowel "a" from the number.

| 2 | thnein | 20 | ^{9}ishriin |
| 3 | tlaatha | 30 | tlaathiin |

4	arba⁹a	40	arba⁹iin
5	khamsa	50	khamsiin
6	sitta	60	sittiin
7	sab⁹a	70	sab⁹iin
8	thmaanya	80	thmaaniin
9	tis⁹a	90	tis⁹iin
100	miyya (new number)		

Numbers between twenty-one and twenty-nine, thirty-one and thirty-nine, and so on are read from right to left, by adding **-wa-** (and) after the first digit.

21	waahid-wa-⁹ishriin
22	thnein-wa-⁹ishriin
23	tlaatha-wa-⁹ishriin
24	arba⁹a-wa-⁹ishriin
25	khamsa-wa-⁹ishriin
26	sitta-wa-⁹ishriin
27	sab⁹a-wa-⁹ishriin
28	thmanya-wa-⁹ishriin
29	tis⁹a-wa-⁹ishriin
30	tlaathiin
31	waahid-wa-tlaathiin
32	thnein-wa-tlaathiin
100	miyya

Counting

When counting, Arabic has three forms: singular, dual, and plural.
Numbers three through ten are followed by plural nouns, while
numbers higher than ten are followed by singular nouns.

Masculine Noun

one lesson	daris (*sing.*)
two lessons	darsein (*dl.*)
three lessons	tlath druus (*pl.*)
four lessons	arba⁹ druus
five lessons	khams druus
six lessons	sitt druus
seven lessons	sab⁹ druus
eight lessons	thman druus
nine lessons	tis⁹ druus
ten lessons	⁹ashr druus
eleven lessons	da⁹ash daris (*sing.*)
twelve lessons	thna⁹sh daris

Feminine Noun

one car	sayyaara (*sing.*)
two cars	sayyaartein (*dl.*)
three cars	tlath syyaaraat (*pl.*)
four cars	arba⁹ sayyaaraat
five cars	khamis sayyaaraat
eleven cars	da⁹ash sayyaara (*sing.*)

Ordinal Numbers

first	awwal
second	thaani
third	thaalith
fourth	raabi⁹
fifth	<u>kh</u>aamis
sixth	saadis
seventh	saabi⁹
eighth	thaamin
ninth	taasi⁹
tenth	⁹aashir

first lesson	awwal daris
second lesson	thaani daris
third lesson	thaalith daris

Time

Basic Words and Phrases

and	wa, w-
before	illa, gabul
day/s	yoom/ayyaam
future	mustaqbal
half	nus<u>s</u>
hour/s, time, watch	saa⁹a/saa⁹aat
last, past	faat
minute/s	daqiiqa/daqaayiq
month/s	shahar/ashhur

31

next, coming	jaay
past	maazi
present	haazir
quarter	rubu⁹
season/s	fasil/fusuul
shall, will, going to	rah-, ha-
week/s	usbuu⁹/asaabii⁹
year/s	sana/sniin

Telling Time (il-waqit)

What time is it, please?	rajaa'an, ibbeish is-saa⁹a?
The time is one o'clock.	is-saa⁹a wihda.
two o'clock.	*thintein.*
three o'clock.	*tlaatha.*
four o'clock.	*arba⁹a.*
five o'clock.	*khamsa.*
six o'clock.	*sitta.*
seven o'clock.	*sab⁹a.*
eight o'clock.	*thmaanya.*
nine o'clock.	*tis⁹a.*
ten o'clock.	*⁹ashra.*
eleven o'clock.	*da⁹ash.*
twelve o'clock.	*thna⁹ash.*
The time is 1:10.	is-saa⁹a wihda w ⁹ashra.
1:15.	*wihda w rubu⁹.*
1:20.	*wihda w thilith.*
1:30.	*wihda w nuss.*
12:40.	*wihda illa thilith.*

12:45.	*wihda illa rubu⁹.*
12:50.	*wihda illa ⁹ashra.*
12:55.	*wihda illa khamsa.*

Parts of the Day (aqsaam il-yoom)

morning	sabaahan, subuh
noon	zuhran, zuhur
early afternoon	⁹asran, ⁹asir
late afternoon	masaa'an, masaa'
night	leilan, leil
middle of the night	nuss il-leil

When telling time in Iraqi Arabic, one should follow the actual time with the time of day.

What time are you coming?	shwakit rah-tiji?
I will come at 5:00 P.M.	rah-aji is-saa⁹a khamsa l-⁹asir.
I will come at 10:00 A.M.	rah-aji is-saa⁹a ⁹ashra s-subuh.

Days of the Week (ayyaam li-sbuu⁹)

What day is today?	shunu il-yoom?
Today is Monday.	il-yoom li-thnein.
Tuesday.	*ith-thalaathaa.*
Wednesday.	*il-arbal-⁹aa'.*
Thursday.	*il-khamiis.*
Friday. (Iraqi weekend day)	*il-jum⁹a.*

Saturday.	*is-sabit.*
Sunday.	*il-ahhad.*
How many days in the week?	kam yoom bil-usbuu⁹?
There are seven days.	sabi⁹ tiyyaam.

Months of the Year (ashhur is-sana)

What month is it?	ay shahar haadha?
It is the month of January.	haadha shahar Kaanuun ith-Thaani.
February.	*Shbaat.*
March.	*Aadhaar.*
April.	*Niisaan.*
May.	*Maayis.*
June.	*Huzayraan.*
July.	*Tammuuz.*
August.	*Aab.*
September.	*Ayluul.*
October.	*Tishriin il-Awwal.*
November.	*Tishriin ith-Thaani.*
December.	*Kaanuun il-Awwal.*
How many months in the year?	kam shahar bil-sana?
There are twelve months.	thna⁹ash shahar.

The Four Seasons (fuṣuul is-sana)

Which season is it?	ay fasil haadha?
It is spring.	haadha fasil ir-Rabii⁹.
summer.	*is-Seif.*

34

autumn., fall.	*il-Khariif.*
winter.	*ish-Shita.*
I will travel in the spring.	rah̲-asaafir bir-Rabii⁹.

Past, Present, and Future Expressions

Past (il-maaz̲i)

yesterday	il-baar̲ha
yesterday afternoon	il-baar̲ha l-⁹asir
day before yesterday	awwal il-baar̲ha
last week	li-sbuu⁹ il-faat̲
last month	ish-shahar il-faat
last year	is-sana l-faatat
I didn't see you yesterday.	ma-shiftak il-baar̲ha.

Present (il-h̲aazir)

now	hissa
today	il-yoom
this week	haad̲ha l-usbuu⁹
this month	haad̲ha sh-shahar
this year	haad̲hi s-sana
this year in the spring	haad̲hi s-sana bir-Rabii⁹
I am leaving now.	raayih̲ hissa.

Future (il-mustaqbal)

tomorrow	baachir
day after tomorrow	⁹ugub baachir

next week	li-sbuu⁹ il-jaay
next month	ish-shahar il-jaay
next year	is-sana l-jaayya
a week from today	ba⁹ad usbuu⁹
an hour from now	ba⁹ad saa⁹a
tomorrow night	baachir bil-leil

I will see you tomorrow night.	ra<u>h</u>-ashuufak baachir bil-leil.

Holidays and Festivals (⁹u_tal wa a⁹yaad)

In Iraq, as in all countries, people celebrate religious and national holidays. Religious holidays are universal all over the Arab and Islamic world, whereas national holidays vary from one country to another. Friday is the official weekend holiday in Iraq.

Religious Holidays (⁹u_tal diiniyya)

The dates of the Islamic holidays are based on the Islamic Hijra calendar, which is a lunar system. Thus these dates change from year to year in relation to the Gregorian calendar. Religious holidays in Iraq are as follows:

Al-Fitr Festival/the Small Festival (⁹iid al-Fi_tr/⁹iid al-Sa<u>gh</u>iir). A major three-day festival occurring at the end of the month of Ramadan, when Muslims refrain from eating and drinking from dawn to sunset every day.

The Sacrificial Festival/the Big Festival (⁹iid al-A̱zha/⁹iid al-Kabiir). A major four-day festival follows the pilgrimage (ẖajj) to the holy city of Mecca in Saudi Arabia. The name of this festival comes from the ritual act of every pilgrim sacrificing a lamb at the end of the ẖajj.

Muslim New Year's Day (⁹iid Raas is-Sana)

Prophet Muhammad's Birthday (⁹iid Mawlid in-Nabi)

Ashoura Day (Yoom ⁹aashuura). The Shiite Muslims commemorate this day in memory of the martyr Imam al-Hussein, grandson of the Prophet Muhammad.

Christian New Year's Day (⁹iid Raas is-Sana)

National Holidays (⁹utal wa̱taniyya)

- Iraqi Army Day (Yoom i̱j-Jaysh il-⁹iraaqi), January 6
- Spring Day (Yoom in-Nawruuz), March 21
- Overthrown Saddam's Day (⁹iid it-Ta̱kha̱llus̱ min Saddaam), April 9 (new national holiday in 2003)
- Labor Day (Yoom il-⁹umaal), May 1
- 1958 Revolution Anniversary (Yoom Arbaata̱⁹sh Tammuuz), July 14

Weather (il-jaww)

Weather in Iraq varies geographically among the southern, central, and northern sectors. In general, summers are hot and temperatures can reach 120°F/50°C; winters are cold and temperatures may fall below zero. In the spring and fall, temperatures are moderate and pleasant.

Basic Words and Phrases

clouds	g̲huyuum
cold	baarid
dry	jaaf
dust	⁹ajaaj
dust storm	⁹aasifa turaabiyya
hot	h̲aar
humid	ratub
moderate	mu⁹tadil
moon	gumar
rain	mut̲ar
snow	thalij
sun	shamis
temperature	darajat il-har̲aara
warm	daafi
weather	jaww, manaak̲h̲
wind	riyaah̲

How is the weather today?	shloon ij-jaww il-yoom?
It's hot.	il-yoom h̲aara.
It's cold.	il-yoom baarda.
It's humid.	il-yoom ratuba.
It's neither hot nor cold.	il-yoom laa h̲aara wala baarda.
There's dust.	aku ⁹ajaaj.
It's moderate.	il-yoom mu⁹tadil.
It's raining.	il-yoom mut̲ar.
It's windy.	il-yoom aku riyaah̲.
It's cloudy.	il-yoom mg̲hayma.
It's sunny.	il-yoom mshamsa.

What's the temperature today?	shgadd darajat il-<u>h</u>araara il-yoom?
What's the weather going to be like next week?	shloon rah-ykuun ij-jaww lis-buu⁹ ij-jaay?
next month?	*ish-shahar ij-jaay?*
Summer is hot in Iraq.	is-<u>S</u>eif <u>h</u>arr bil-⁹iraaq.
Winter is cold in Iraq.	ish-Shita baarid bil-⁹iraaq.
Fall is moderate in Iraq.	il-<u>Kh</u>ariif mu⁹tadil bil-⁹iraaq.

Colors (alwaan)

black	aswad
blue	azrag
brown	joozi, asmar
dark	<u>t</u>oo<u>kh</u>, <u>gh</u>aamuq
gray	rumaadi
green	a<u>kh</u> zar
light	faati<u>h</u>
navy	niili
orange	purtuqaali
pink	wardi
purple	banafsaji
red	a<u>h</u>mar
white	abya<u>z</u>
yellow	a<u>s</u>far

39

Weights and Measures (qiyaasaat wa awzaan)

The metric system is used in Iraq, although U.S. measures can also be translated.

centimeter	santimatir
inch	inch
meter	matir
mile	miil
yard	yaard
gram	ghraam
kilo	keilo
kilogram	keilo ghraam
kilometer	keilomatir
liter	latir
half	nuss
quarter	rubu⁹
half a kilo	nuss keilo

| a quarter kilo | rubu⁹ keilo |
| a liter of water | latir mayy |

| The hotel is one kilometer away. | il-findiq ⁹ala bu⁹ud keilomatir. |

Common Signs

The following are some of the common signs that travelers are likely to see in Iraq.

Airport	مطار
Arrival	وصول
Bus	باص
Cashier	صراف
Caution	احذر
Closed	مغلوق
Crossing	عبور
Danger	خطر
Departure	مغادرة
Discount, Sale	تنزيلات
Don't touch	لا تلمس
Don't walk	لا تمشي
Elevator	مصعد
Entrance	دخول

Exit	خروج
For rent	للإيجار
For sale	للبيع
Forbidden	ممنوع
Men's room	للرجال
Museum	متحف
No bathing	ممنوع السباحة
No parking	ممنوع الوقوف
No smoking	ممنوع التدخين
Open	مفتوح
Private	خاص
Public	عام
Reserved	محجوز
Stop	قف
Street	شارع
Taxi	تكسي
Toilet	تواليت
Train	قطار
Vacant	خالي
Waiting room	غرفة انتظار
Walk, Cross	امشي
Women only	للنساء فقط
Women's room	للنساء

Chapter **3**

General Phrases

Traveling to Iraq

At the Airport (bil-mataar)

airlines	k̲h̲utuut tayyaraan
Iraqi Airlines	*K̲h̲utuut it-Tayyaraan il-⁹iraaqiyya*
Lufthansa Airlines	*K̲h̲utuut Tayyaraan Lufthansa*
airplane	tayyaara
arrival	wusuul
Baghdad International Airport	Mataar Bag̲h̲daad id-Diwali
canceling	ilg̲h̲aa'
changing	tag̲h̲yiir
confirming a reservation	ta'kiid hajiz
currency exchange office	maktab tasriif
customs	gumrug
departure	mug̲h̲aadara
duty-free shop	mak̲h̲zan is-suuq il-hurra
flight check-in desk	maktab tasjiil ir-rihla

inspection	taftiish
luggage	junta
passport	paasport, jawaaz
plane	tayyaara
porter	hammaal
tip	bakh shiish

On Arrival (wusuul)

Where is passport control?	wein qisim il-paasport?
Where is customs control?	wein qisim il-gumrug?
Where is my luggage?	wein junutti?
Where is my passport?	wein paasporti?
I have no illegal items.	maa ⁹indi ashyaa' mamnuu⁹a.
I have nothing to declare.	maa ⁹indi shii a⁹ilna.
I have gifts and personal items.	⁹indi hadaayaa wa ashyaa' shakh siyya.
Do I have to pay duty?	laazim adfa ⁹gumrug?
Can I close my bag?	mumkin asidd junutti?
My bag is blue.	junutti zarga.
brown.	*jooziyya.*
green.	*khazra.*
khaki.	*khaaki.*
red.	*hamra.*
I arrived on . . . airlines.	wisalit ⁹ala khutuut . . .
I am here on an official visit.	aani hnaa bi-ziyaara rasmiyya.
I am here as a tourist.	aani hnaa saa'ih.
I am just passing through.	aani hnaa ⁹ubuur.
I am staying for one week.	aani baaqi usbuu⁹.

I am staying at the Qanat Hotel.	aani naazil b-Findiq il-Qanaat.
I want a currency exchange office, please.	rajaa'an, ariid maktab tasriif.
Please change $50.	rajaa'an, sarrufli khamsiin duulaar.
I want a taxi, please.	rajaa'an, ariid taksi.
Please take me to . . . hotel.	rajaa'an, khudhni l-findiq . . .
How much is the fare?	shgadd il-ujra?

On Departure (mughaadara)

Where is Lufthansa Airlines, please?	rajaa'an, wein Khutuut Tayyaraan Lufthansa?
Over there.	hnaak.
Is this Lufthansa?	haadhi Lufthansa?
Yes.	na⁹am., 'ii.
I have a reservation on flight 110.	⁹indi hajiz ⁹ar-rihla 110.
I have a first-class ticket.	⁹indi bitaaqa daraja uulaa.
I have an economy-class ticket.	⁹indi bitaaqa daraja siyaahiyya.
I have a business-class ticket.	⁹indi bitaaqa darajat rajul a⁹maal.
What is the departure time?	shwakit waqt il-mughaadara?
When is the arrival?	shwakit il-wusuul?
What is the gate number?	shunu raqam il-bawwaaba?
This is my luggage.	haadhi junati.
I'd like a window seat, please.	rajaa'an ahibb kursi yamm shubbaak.
With pleasure. (reply)	iddallal.

Have a good trip.	rihla sa⁹iida.
Thank you.	shukran.

Getting a Porter (hammaal)

Where are the luggage carts?	wein ⁹arabaanaat ij-junat?
My luggage is heavy.	junati thigiila.
I need a porter.	ariid hammal.
This is my luggage.	haadhi junati.
Be careful with those bags.	diir baalak ⁹aj-junat.
It's very heavy.	hiyya thigiila hwaaya.
There is a bag missing.	aku junta naaqsa.
Please ask the officer over there.	rajaa'an, ruuh is'al il-muwazzaf hnaak.
It's black.	hiyya sooda.
Please hurry!	b-sur⁹a rajaa'an!
Get me a taxi, please.	hassilli taksi, rajaa'an.
How much is the fee?	shgadd il-ujra?
Here is the fee.	tfazzal il-ujra.
Thank you.	shukran.
Good-bye.	ma⁹a s-slaama.

Accommodations

Basic Words and Phrases

address	⁹inwaan
bathroom	hammaam
bed	siriir

double bed	siriir mizdawaj
downtown	markaz il-madiina
expensive	ghaali
hotel, motel	findiq
inexpensive, cheap	rikhiis
key	miftaah
lavatory, toilet	mirhaaz, twaaleit
National Tourist Bureau	Maktab is-Siyaaha il-Watani
Qanat Hotel	Findiq il-Qanaat
Rashid Hotel	Findiq ir-Rashiid
reservation	hajiz
room	ghurfa
large room	*ghurfa chbiira*
small room	*ghurfa zghayra*
room service	khidmat il-ghuraf
shower	duush
water	mayy
cold water	*mayy baarid*
hot water	*mayy haar*

Finding a Hotel

Where is a good hotel?	wein aku findiq zein?
not very expensive	muu kullish ghaali
downtown	b-markaz il-madiina
in a good location	b-mawqi⁹ zein
Is the Rashid Hotel a good one?	Findiq ir-Rashiid zein?
What is the address?	shunu ⁹inwaana?
Please write down the address.	rajaa'an, iktibli ⁹inwaana.

47

Take me to the hotel, please.	khudhni lil-findiq, min fazlak.
Which bus goes to the hotel?	ay paas yruuh lil-findiq?

At the Hotel: Checking In (nuzuul)

Hello.	marhaba.
You are welcome. (reply)	ahlan wa sahlan.
My name is . . .	ismi . . .
Here is my passport.	tfazzal paasporti.
Thank you. (reply)	shukran.
I have a reservation.	9indi hajiz.
I do not have a reservation.	maa 9indi hajiz.
I want a room with a double bed and bath.	ariid ghurfa ma9a siriir mizdawaj wa hammaam.
without a bath.	*biduun hammaam.*
What is the room price?	shgadd si9ir il-ghurfa?
I am staying one week.	aani baaqi usbuu9.
Shall I fill in this form?	laazim amli haadhi l-istimaara?
May I see the room, please?	mumkin ashuuf il-ghurfa, min fazlak?
The room is good.	il-ghurfa zeina.
The room is not good.	il-ghurfa muu zeina.
Why?	leish?
It's very small.	zghayra hwaaya.
I want a better room.	ariid ghurfa ahsan.
a bigger room.	*ghurfa akbar.*
a cleaner room.	*ghurfa anzaf.*
a smaller room.	*ghurfa as-ghar.*
Where is the elevator?	wein il-mas9ad?

Somebody help me with the luggage, please.	ahhad ysaa⁹idni bil-junat, min fazlak.
Is there a restaurant in the hotel?	aku mat⁹am bil-findiq?

Checking Out (mughaadara)

Good morning.	sabaah il-kheir.
Good morning. (reply)	sabaah in-nuur.
I'd like to check out.	ahibb aghaadir.
Here is the room key.	tfazzal miftaah il-ghurfa.
The bill, please.	rajaa'an li-hsaab.
May I pay with a credit card?	mumkin adfa⁹ b-taaqat li-'timaan?
with a traveler's check?	*b-shiik siyaahi?*
Yes.	na⁹am.
There is a mistake in the bill.	aku ghalat bli-hsaab.
What mistake? (reply)	ay ghalat?
May I leave my luggage here until this afternoon?	mumkin atruk junati hnaa hatta l-⁹asir?
Yes, with pleasure.	na⁹am, ⁹ala ⁹eini.
Please get me a taxi.	rajaa'an, hassilli taksi.
Good-bye.	ma⁹a s-salaama.

Requests, Queries, and Problems

Where is the bar?	wein il-baar?
elevator?	*il-mas⁹ad?*
lavatory?	*li-twaaleit?*
parking lot?	*mawqif is-sayyaaraat?*
restaurant?	*il-mat⁹am?*

Is there a laundry?	aku makwa?
a money changer?	*sarraaf?*
a pool?	*masbah?*
a telephone?	*talafoon?*
What time is breakfast?	shwakit il-futuur?
lunch?	*il-ghada?*
dinner?	*il-⁹asha?*
Bring me tea, please.	jiibli chaay, rajaa'an.
Bring me coffee, please.	jiibli gahwa, rajaa'an.
Are there letters for me?	aku rasaa'il ili?
Do you have dry cleaning in the hotel?	⁹idkum ghasil wa kawi bil-findiq?
Is there a post office?	aku bariid?
Is there a mailbox?	aku sanduuq bariid?
I need another blanket.	ariid battaaniy thaanya.
another pillow.	*mkhadda thaanya.*
another towel.	*khaawli thaani.*
soap.	*saabuun.*
Could you wake me up at . . . ?	mumkin tsahhiini s-saa⁹a . . . ?
May I put this in the safe?	mumkin atruk haadhi bil-qaasa?
The room is hot.	il-ghurfa haara.
cold.	*baarda.*
Sorry, the key is lost.	mit'assif, zaa⁹ il-miftaah.
There is no hot water in my room.	maaku mayy haar b-ghurfti.
There is no electricity in my room.	maaku kahrabaa' b-ghurfti.
Thank you.	shukran.

Getting Around

Basic Words and Phrases

address	⁹inwaan
airport	mataar
beside, adjacent to	yamm
bus	paas
cinema	ciinama
corner	zaawiya
far	bi⁹iid
gas	baanziin
gas station	baanziinkhaana
go	ruuh, imshi
hotel	findiq
How far?	shgadd bi⁹iid?
map	khariita
market	suug
museum	mathaf
Iraqi Museum (the)	*il-Mathaf il-⁹iraaqi*
nearby, close by	qariib, yamm
park	muntazah
please	rajaa'an, min fazlak
sign	⁹alaama
square	saaha
station	mahatta
street	shaari⁹
taxi stop, stand	mawqif
train	qitaar
Where?	wein?

Asking for Directions and Places

I don't know how to go to . . .	maa andal shloon aruuh ilaa . . .
Where is the train station, please?	rajaa'an, wein mahattat il-qitaar?
Where is the bus stop, please?	rajaa'an, wein mawqif il-paas?
Where is the taxi stop, please?	rajaa'an, wein mawqif il-taksi?
I want a private taxi.	ariid taksi khususi.
I want a public taxi.	ariid taksi nafaraat.
Are you free?	inta faarigh?
Please take me to the airport.	rajaa'an, khudhni li-lmataar.
this address.	*l-haadha l⁹inwaan.*
this hotel.	*l-haadha l-findiq.*
the train station.	*il-mahattat il-qitaar.*
How much is the fare?	shgadd il-ujra?
This is too much.	haadha ghaali.
Please go faster. I'm in a hurry.	rajaa'an, b-sur⁹a. aani mista⁹jil.
Please slow down.	rajaa'an, suuq ⁹ala keifak.
You are going the wrong way.	inta raayih bit-tariiq il-ghalat.
Please take the fare.	tfazzal il-ujra.
Which bus should I take to go to this address?	ay paas aakhudh l-haadha l-⁹inwaan?
this cinema?	*l-haadhi s-siinama?*
this hotel?	*l-haadha l-findiq?*
this street?	*l-haadha sh-shaari⁹?*
What bus number?	ay raqam paas?
How many stops?	kam mawqif?
Please tell me when we get there.	rajaa'an, gulli laman noosal.
Do you have a map of the city?	⁹indak khariitat il-madiina?
Close by or far away?	qariib loo bi⁹iid?
How far?	shgadd bi⁹iid?

Where is a bank?	wein aku bank?
a gas station?	*aku baanziinkhaana?*
the Iraqi Museum?	*il-Mathaf il-⁹iraaqi?*
a nearby mailbox?	*aku sanduuq bariid?*
a post office?	*aku bariid?*
the Qanat Hotel?	*Findiq il-Qanaat?*
the Safafir Market? (famous	*Suug is-Safaafiir?*
market in Baghdad)	
the Shorja Market? (famous	*Suug ish-Shoorja?*
market in Baghdad)	
the Tahriir Square? (downtown	*Saahat it-Tahriir?*
Baghdad)	
a travel office?	*aku maktab safar?*

Traveling

Basic Words and Phrases

airlines	khutuut tayyaraan
airplane	tayyaara
bus	paas
driver's license	ijaazat siyaaqa
international	*⁹aalamiyya*
from . . . to . . .	min . . . ilaa . . .
How much?	shgadd?
information office	maktab isti⁹laamaat
insurance	ta'miin
National Tourist Bureau	Maktab is-Siyaaha il-Watani
nonsmoking section	qisim ⁹adam it-tadkhiin

number	raqam
one way	d̲hihaaban
please	rajaa'an
round-trip	murajja⁹, d̲hihaaban wa iyaaban
smoking section	qisim it-tad̲k̲hiin
taxi	taksi
private taxi (hired by one person)	*taksi k̲husus̲i*
public taxi (shared by several individuals)	*taksi nafraat*
ticket	tad̲hkara, tikit
tourism office	maktab siyaah̲i
train	qitaar
travel office, agency	maktak safar

Buying Travel Tickets (shiraa' tikit safar)

I want a bus ticket, please.	rajaa'an, ariid tikit paas̲.
a train ticket	*tikit qitaar.*
an airline ticket.	*tikit t̲ayyaara.*
from here to Basra	min hnaa lil-Basra
Musil	*lil-Muusil*
Babylon	*il-Baabil*
round-trip	murajja⁹
one way only	d̲hihaaban bass
first class	daraja uulaa
economy class	daraja siyaah̲iyya
I'd like a window seat.	ahibb maq⁹ad yamm ish-shubbaak.

I'd like a seat in the smoking section.	ahibb maq⁹ad b-qisim il-tadkhiin.
nonsmoking section.	*qisim ⁹adam it-tadkhiin.*
What is the flight number?	shunu raqam ir-rihla?
bus number?	*raqam il-paas?*
train number?	*raqam il-qitaar?*
Where is the information office?	wein maktab l-isti⁹laamaat?
Where is the waiting room?	wein ghurfat l-intizaar?
What time does the plane leave?	beish is-saa⁹a tghaadir it-tayyaara?
train?	*il-qitaar?*
bus?	*il-paas?*
They say the plane is late.	yguuluun it-tayyaara mitakhra.
Why is it late?	leish mitakhra?
When shall we arrive?	shwakit rah-noosal?
These are my bags.	haadhi junati.
Thank you.	shukran.

Banking and Money Matters

The monetary unit of Iraq is the dinar, which is divided into one thousand fils. Although you may get better exchange rates on the black market, it's advisable to make all money transactions in banks or authorized currency exchange offices.

Basic Words and Phrases

automated teller, cash machine	aalat sahb fluus
bank	bank, masraf

Central Bank	*il-Bank il-Markazi*
Rafidain Bank	*Bank ir-Raafidein*
black market	suuq sooda
check	sakk, chakk
bad check	*chakk muu zein*
good check	*chakk zein*
personal check	*chakk shakh si*
traveler's checks	*sheikaat siyaahiyya*
checking account	hsaab jaari
credit card	butaaqat i'timaan, butaaqat
	credit card
currency	⁹umla
hard currency	*⁹umla sa⁹ba*
currency exchange office	maktab tasriif
dinar (Iraqi currency)	diinaar
one quarter of a dinar	*rubu⁹ diinaar*
one half of a dinar	*nuss diinaar*
exchange rate	si⁹ir it-tasriif
financial	maali
money	fluus
American money	*fluus Amriikiyya*
European money	*fluus Awrubbiyya*
Iraqi money	*fluus ⁹iraaqiyya*
Italian money	*fluus Itaaliyya*
penny	filis
please	rajaa'an
savings account	hsaab tawfiir
small change	khurda
teller, cashier	sarraaf

At the Bank (bil-bank)

Please, where is the Rafidain Bank?	rajaa'an, wein Bank ir-Raafidein?
Central Bank?	*il-Bank il-Markazi?*
I'd like to change money in dollars.	ahibb asarruf fluus bil-dulaaraat.
in Euros.	*bil-yooro.*
in traveler's checks.	*sheikaat siyaahiyya.*
What is the exchange rate?	shgadd si⁹ir it-tasriif?
Can I get money with my credit card?	mumkin as-hab fluus bil-kradit kard maali?
Can I have money transferred here from my bank?	mumkin ahawwil fluus hnaa min il bank maali?
Can I cash a personal check?	agdar asarruf chak shakh si?
I've lost my traveler's checks.	zayya⁹it sheikaati is-siyaahiyya.
These are their numbers.	haadhi arqaamha.
Is there a cash machine?	aku aala li-sahb li-fluus?
I could not use my credit card.	ma-gdarit ashab fluus bil-card.
When does the bank open?	shwakit yftah il-bank?
What time does the bank close?	shwakit yughluq il-bank?
Thanks.	shukran.

Postage and Communication

Basic Words and Phrases

address	⁹unwaan
airmail	bariid jawwi
amount	mablagh

envelope	zaruf
airmail envelope	*zaruf jawwi*
express mail	bariid sarii⁹
How much?	shgadd?
letter	risaala
mail	bariid
mailbox	sanduuq bariid
mailman	abu l-bariid, bos tachi
money orders	hawaala maaliyya
package	ruzma
postal orders	hawaala bariidiyya
postcard	postkaart
post office	maktab bariid
receipt	wasil
registered letter	risaala musajjala
regular mail	bariid ⁹aadi
stamp/s	taabi⁹/tawaabi⁹

At the Post Office (bil-bariid)

I want to mail a letter.	ariid adiz risaala.
Where is a post office?	wein aku bariid?
Where is a mailbox?	wein aku sanduuq bariid?
Is this the stamp window?	haadha shubbaak it-tawaabi⁹?
I want stamps for a letter to France.	ariid tawaabi⁹ li-risaala li-Fransa.
I want stamps for a postcard.	ariid tawaabi⁹ li-postkaart.
I want a money order for $1,000.	ariid hawaala bariidiyya b-mablagh alif duulaar.

I want to mail this package to England.	ariid adiz haadhi r-ruzma ilaa Ingiltara.
to the United States.	*ilaa Amriika.*
by express mail.	*bil-bariid is-sarii⁹.*
by airmail.	*bil-bariid ij-jawwi.*
How much is it?	shgadd?
Please give me a receipt.	rajaa'an intiini waṣil.
Thanks.	shukran.

Calling, Faxing, and Copying

busy	mashghuul
copier	aalat istinsaakh, ziiroks
fax	faaks
international call	mukaalama khaarijiyya, mukaalam duwaliyya
Internet	intarnat
line	khatt
local call	mukaalama daakhiliyya
minute	daqiiqa
number	raqam
operator	baddaala
telephone	talafoon
telephone call	mukaalama, mukhaabara
wrong	ghalat
Is there a telephone here?	aku talafoon hnaa?
Is there a fax here?	aku faaks hnaa?

I'd like to make an international call.	ahibb asawwi mukaalama khaarijiyya.
to Amman.	*ilaa ⁹ammaan.*
How much is one minute?	shgadd id-daqiiqa?
How can I get the operator?	shloon ahassil il-baddaala?
Operator, can you please get me number . . . ?	baddaala, mumkin min fazlak thassilli raqam . . . ?
Thank you.	shukran.
My number is . . .	raqmi . . .
May I speak to . . . ?	mumkin atkallam wiyya . . . ?
I can't hear you.	maa agdar asim⁹ak.
The line is busy.	il-khatt mashghuul.
Wrong number.	raqam ghalat.
There is no answer.	maaku jawaab.
Could you reconnect me?	mumkin thasilli ir-raqam marra thaanya?
The phone is not working.	it-talafoon kharbaan.
May I have a wake-up call for . . . o'clock, please?	mumkin tga⁹idni is-saa⁹a . . . min fazlak?
May I reserve time for a call at . . . o'clock?	mumkin ahjiz mukhaabara is-saa⁹a . . . ?
Thank you.	shukran.

Automotive

Cars drive on the right-hand side of the road in Iraq, and international traffic signs are used. If you are planning to drive in Iraq, you must buy auto insurance from the Iraqi National Insurance Company, and you should have an international driver's license issued in your country of origin.

Basic Words and Phrases

air	hawa, hawaa'
battery	baatri
brakes	breikaat
flat tire	panchar
gas	baanziin
gas station	mahattat baanziin, baanziinkhaana
highway	tariiq sarii9
in a hurry	mista9jil
later	ba9dein
lavatory, toilet	mirhaaz, twaaleit
left	yisra, yisaar
lights	azwiya
little	shwayya
mechanic	miikaaniiki
mechanic's shop, garage	mahal miikaaniiki
much	hwaaya
must, should	laazim
National Insurance Company	Sharikat il-Ta'miin il-Wataniyya
now	hissa
oil	dihin
or	loo
please	rajaa'an, min fazlak
price, cost	si9ir
pump	mazakhkha, pamp

right	yimna, yamiin
road	tariiq
straight	9adil
street	shaari9

Renting a Car (ta'jiir sayyaara)

I want to rent a car, please.	rajaa'an, ariid ta'jiir sayyaara.
I want an American car.	ariid sayyaara Amriikiyya.
a Japanese car.	*sayyaara Yaabaaniyya.*
I don't care about the color.	ma-yhimni il-loon.
For how many days?	kam yoom?
One day.	*yoom waahid.*
Two days.	*yoomein.*
Three days.	*tlath tiyyaam.*
Four days.	*arba9 tiyyaam.*
One week.	*usbuu9 waahid.*
Two weeks.	*usbuu9ein.*
How much is the fare?	shgadd il-ujra?
This is too expensive.	haadha ghaali hwaaya.
I have an international driver's license.	9indi ijaazat siyaaqa 9aalamiyya.
Do you have car insurance?	9idkum ta'miin sayyaaraat?
We have two drivers.	ihna saayqein.
May I have a driver with the car?	mumkin ta'jiir saayiq wiyya is-sayyaara?
Do you have an office in another city?	9idkum maktab b-madiina thaanya?
May I return the car to another city?	mumkin arajji9 is-sayyaara b-madiina thaanya?

May I see the car?	mumkin ashuuf is-sayyaara?
I want a car with an automatic transmission.	ariid sayyaara otomaatikiyya.
May I stop/park the car here?	mumkin awagguf is-sayyaara hnaa?
I'm having problems with the car.	⁹indi ⁹a̱tal bis-sayyaara.

On the Road (fi̱t-̱tariiq)

I'm lost.	aani zaayi⁹.
Please tell me the way to the Rashid Hotel.	rajaa'an, gulli ay ̱tariiq il-Findiq ir-Rashiid.
Should I go right or left?	aruu̱h yisra loo yimna?
or straight?	*loo ⁹adil?*
Should I take the highway?	aa̱khudh it-̱tariiq is-sarii⁹?
Where is the main street?	wein ish-shaari⁹ ir-ra'iisi?
How far away is it?	shgadd bi⁹iid?
Can you show it to me on the map?	mumkin tshawwifni ⁹al-̱khariita?
Is this a good road?	haa̱dha ̱tariiq zein?
Where is the next gas station?	wein aku baanziiṉkhaana thaanya?

At the Gas Station (baanziiṉkhaana)

Hello, please . . .	maṟhaba, min fazlak . . .
Fill the car up with premium (gas).	⁹abbi s-sayyaara baanziin mumtaaz.
regular (gas).	*⁹aadi.*

Please, check the oil.	min fazlak, ifhass id-dihin.
the tires.	it-taayaraat.
Where is the air pump?	wein mazakhkhat il-hawa?
Where is the lavatory?	wein il-mirhaaz?

Problems and Repair (mashaakil wa tasliih)

I need a mechanic's shop.	mihtaaj mahal miikaaniiki.
My car has broken down.	sayyaarti khurbat.
Can you help me, please?	mumkin tsaa⁹idni, min fazlak?
Can you give me a push?	mumkin tidfa⁹ sayyaarti?
Check the car, please.	ifhass is-sayyaara, rajaa'an.
The car is overheated.	is-sayyaara himat hwaaya.
The car doesn't start.	is-sayyaara ma-tushtughul.
I have a flat tire.	⁹indi panchar.
I ran out of gas.	khilas il-baanziin.
The battery is dead.	il-baatri mayyit.
There are no brakes.	maaku breikaat.
There are no lights.	maaku azwiya.
The windshield is broken.	missaahaat ij-jaam kharbaana.
The engine suddenly stopped.	il-muharrik wugaf ⁹ala ghafla.
I forgot the keys inside the car.	nseit il-mafaatiih bis-sayyaara.
Do you have a phone?	⁹indak talafoon?
I want to call my company.	ariid akhaabur sharikti.
Can you repair the car?	mumkin tsallih is-sayyaara?
How long will it take to repair?	shgadd taakhudh waqit lil-tasliih?
Can you fix it quickly?	mumkin tsallih is-sayyaara b-sur⁹a?

I am in a hurry.	aani mista⁹jil.
How much does it cost?	shgadd il-kilfa?
This is too much.	haadha ghaali hwaaya.
Reduce the price a little!	qallil is-si⁹ir shwayya!

Accidents (haadith)

accident	haadith, is tiidaam
car accident	*haadith sayyaara*
ambulance	sayyaarat is⁹aaf
car license	raqam is-sayyaara
doctor	diktoor
driver's license	ijaazat siyaaqa
insurance company	sharakit ta'miin
police station	markaz shurta

I had a car accident.	saar ⁹indi haadith sayyaara.
Where is a telephone?	wein aku talafoon?
I was not driving fast.	ma-chinit asuuq b-sur⁹a.
I want the police to come.	ariid ish-shurta tiji.
I want to go to the police station.	ariid aruuh l-markaz ish-shurta.
People are injured.	aku naas musaabiin.
Do not move him.	la-tharka.
Can you help, please?	mumkin tsaa⁹idni, rajaa'an?
He hit my car.	huwwa sidamni.
He is a witness.	huwwa shaahid.
I do not speak Arabic.	maa atkallam ⁹arabi.
I want an interpreter.	ariid mutarjim.

Parking (mawqif sayyaaraat)

Where can I park the car?	wein agdar awagguf is-sayyaara?
Is there a parking place?	aku mawqif sayyaaraat?
Can I park it on the street?	agdar awagguf is-sayyaara bish-shaari⁹?
I must leave the car now.	laazim atruk is-sayyaara hissa.
I will return later.	rah-arja⁹ ba⁹dein.
Thank you.	shukran.

Food and Drink

Iraqi cuisine is essentially Mediterranean in nature, but it displays a large variety of influences, including Indian, Persian, Turkish, British, and American. No stay in Iraq is complete without eating the famous Baghdadi Masguf, which is river fish caught fresh daily and kept alive in a tank. After you choose your fish, it's grilled on an open fire of tamarisk wood, giving it a delicious flavor.

Basic Words and Phrases

appetizers	mazza
bar	baar
beer	biira
bill	hsaab
breakfast	futuur, rayyuug
café, tea shop	gahwa
casino	gaaziino
delicious	tayyib

dinner, supper	⁹asha
dish/s	akla/aklaat
drink/s	mashurub/mashruubaat
excellent	mumtaaz
expensive	ghaali
food	ta⁹aam, akil
Middle Eastern food	*akil sharqi*
Western food	*akil gharbi*
good-bye	ma⁹a s-salaama
hungry	juu⁹aan
inexpensive	rikhiis
lunch	ghada
market	suug
menu	manyu
please	rajaa'an, min fazlak
reservation	hajiz
restaurant/s	mat⁹am/mataa⁹um
street	shaari⁹
Palestine Street	*Shaari⁹ Filistiin*
Rashid Street	*Shaari⁹ ir-Rashiid*
Saadun Street	*Shaari⁹ is-Sa⁹duun*
thank you, thanks	shukran
thirsty	⁹atshaan
tip	bakhshiish
tomorrow	baachir
tonight	il-leila
traditional food	akil sha⁹bi
waiter	booy

water   mayy
wine   nabii<u>dh</u>

Looking for Restaurants

Do you know a good restaurant?   tu⁹ruf mat⁹am zein?
not very expensive   muu <u>gh</u>aali hwaaya
Does it offer native Iraqi dishes?   yqaddim akil ⁹iraaqi?
Do you know an American   tu⁹ruf mat⁹am
   restaurant?   Amriiki?
   Chinese restaurant?   *mat⁹am Siini?*
   French restaurant?   *mat⁹am Fransi?*
   Indian restaurant?   *mat⁹am Hindi?*
   Italian restaurant?   *mat⁹am Itaali?*
   Lebanese restaurant?   *mat⁹am Lubnaani?*
   Mexican restaurant?   *mat⁹am Maksiiki?*

Restaurant Reservations (<u>h</u>ajiz)

I would like to make a   a<u>h</u>ibb a<u>h</u>jiz lil-⁹asha.
   reservation for dinner.
   lunch.   *lil-<u>gh</u>ada.*
   breakfast.   *lil-ftuur.*
   for two.   *li-thnein.*
   for four.   *l-arba⁹a.*
   for tonight at seven o'clock.   *il-leila is-saa⁹a*
        sab⁹a.

   for tomorrow night at eight   *baachir bil-leil is-saa⁹a*
    o'clock.   *thmaanya.*

At the Restaurant (bil-mat⁹am)

We have a reservation tonight.	⁹idna hajiz il-leila.
You are welcome. (reply)	ahlan wa sahlan.
Have a seat here.	tfazzalu istiriihu hnaa.
Thank you.	shukran.
The menu, please.	il-manyu, rajaa'an.
Do you have a menu in English?	⁹idkum manyu bil-Ingiliizi?
Do you have appetizers?	⁹idkum mazza?
What is today's dish?	shunu aklat il-yoom?
Please bring us appetizers.	rajaa'an jiibilna mazza.
beer.	*biira.*
a bottle of (mineral) water.	*butul mayy.*
drinks.	*mashruub.*
salad.	*zalaata.*
traditional Iraqi food.	*akil ⁹iraaqi sha⁹bi.*
water.	*mayy.*
wine.	*nabiidh.*
Bring us the bill, please.	jiibilna li-hsaab, min fazlak.
Is the tip included in the bill?	il-bakhshiish daakhil bli-hsaab?
The food was excellent.	il-akil kaan mumtaaz.
Thank you very much.	shukran jaziilan.
Good-bye.	ma⁹a s-salaama.

At the Casino/Café (bil-gaziino)

In Baghdad, there are many "casinos" (cafés) on Abu Nuwas Street, long considered the center of Baghdad nightlife, along the Tigris River. The street was named after the famous Arab poet from the eighth century. Some of the most popular Iraqi dishes are served here, among them the famous Masguf fish. It is said that if a "visitor to Baghdad does not eat the Masguf, it is like he has never been to the city."

Abu Nuwas Street	shaari⁹ Abu Nuwaas
also	ayzan, hammein
fish	simach
Masguf fish	simach Masguuf
fresh	taaza
heavy	thigiil
light	khafiif

Where is there a good casino for Masguf?

wein aku gaazino zeina lil-Masguuf?

Do you have fresh fish?

⁹idkum simich taaza?

Make us Masguf fish, please.

sawwilna simich Masguuf, rajaa'an.

   with salad.

   wiyya zalaata.

Bring us Arak (a drink) also.

jiibilna ⁹arag hammein.

The Masguf is a traditional Iraqi dish.

il-Masguuf akla ⁹iraaqiya sha⁹biyya.

Please give me tea.

min fazlak intiini chaay.

   with sugar.

   ma⁹a shakar.

   without sugar.

   biduun shakar.

   light tea.

   chaay khafiif.

   strong tea.

   chaay thigiil.

   coffee with a little sugar.

   gahwa ma⁹a shakar qaliil.

   coffee with milk.

   gahwa ma⁹a haliib.

mineral water.	*butul mayy.*
juice.	*⁹asiir.*
milk.	*ḥaliib.*
The bill, please.	li-ḥsaab, min fazlak.
Good-bye.	ma⁹a s-salaama.

At the Food Market (bis-suug)

Iraqis shop for food (meat, fowl, vegetables, fruit, and so on) in the open market, buying what they need from the various stalls. There are no fixed prices, and bargaining is expected. Don't forget that Iraq uses the metric system (one kilo equals 2.2 pounds).

bag	chiis
bakery	makhbaz, abu il-khubuz
bread (flat)	khubuz
bread (Italian loaf)	sammuun
chicken	dijaaj
fish	simach
fruits	fawaakih
kilo	keilo
half a kilo	*nuṣṣ keilo*
a quarter kilo	*rubu⁹ keilo*
market	suug
food market	*suug khuzrawaat*
price	si⁹ir
vegetables	khuzrawaat

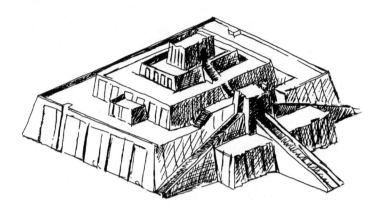

Where is the food market?	wein suug il-<u>kh</u>uzrawaat?
I want to buy meat.	ariid a<u>sh</u>tiri la<u>h</u>am.
Please give me one kilo of meat.	min fazlak, intiini keilo la<u>h</u>am.
How much is one kilo of meat?	ibbei<u>sh</u> keilo il-la<u>h</u>am?
of apples?	*it-tuffaah?*
Please give me one and a half kilos of okra.	min fazlak, intiini keilo w-nuss baamya.
Are the vegetables fresh?	il-<u>kh</u>uzrawaat taaza?
I want a large fish.	ariid simcha chibiira.
I want a small fish.	ariid simcha z<u>gh</u>ayra.
Where is the bakery?	wein abu l-<u>kh</u>ubuz?
Please give me five pieces of bread.	min fazlak, intiini <u>kh</u>amis guras <u>kh</u>ubuz.
Please put the bread in a bag.	min fazlak, <u>kh</u>alli il-<u>kh</u>ubuz bich-chiis.
Would you have somebody help me, please?	⁹indak ahhad ysaa⁹idni', rajaa'an?

Cooking Methods (turuq it-tabukh)

baked	makhbuuz
boiled	masluug
broiled, grilled	mashwi
fried	magli
roasted	mhammar, mashwi
stuffed	mahshi

Meat and Fish (laham wa simich)

chicken	dijaaj
one chicken	*dijaaja*
egg	beiz
one egg	*beiza*
fish	simach
one fish	*simcha*
meat	laham
lamb	*laham ghanam*
beef	*laham baqar*
pork	*laham khanziir*
heart (of sheep)	*galub*
lamb head	*paacha*
liver	*mi⁹laag*

Vegetables (khuzrawaat)

beans (long)	luubya
beets	shwandar
cabbage	lahaana

carrots	jizar
cauliflower	qirnaabiit
corn	dhira
cucumber	khyaar
eggplant	beitinjaan
garlic	thuum
green beans	faasuuliyya khazra
green onion	busal akh zar
lettuce	khass
mushrooms	ftir
okra	baamya
olives	zaytuun
onions	busal
parsley	krafus
peppers (green)	filfildaara
potatoes	poteita
spinach	sbeinaagh
squash	shijar
tomatoes	tamaata
turnips	shalgham
vegetables	khuzrawaat

Fruits (fawaakih)

apples	tuffaah
one apple	*tuffaaha*
apricots	mishmish
bananas	mooz
one banana	*mooza*

cantaloupe	battiikh
one cantaloupe	*battiikha*
dates (palm)	tamur
one date	*tamra*
figs	tiin
one fig	*tiina*
fruits	fawaakih
grapes	9inab
lemons	nuumi haamuz
loquat	langi dinya
mulberries	tukki
oranges	burtuqaal
one orange	*burtuqaala*
peaches	khookh
pears	9armuut
plums	9injaas
pomegranates	rummaan
one pomegranate	*rummaana*
raisins	zbiib
watermelons	raggi
one watermelon	*raggiyya*

Dairy Products and Drinks (albaan wa mashruubaat)

alcoholic drinks	mashruubaat ruuhiyya
butter	zibid
cheese	jibin

coffee	gahwa
Arabic coffee	*gahwa ⁹arabiyya*
Turkish coffee	*gahwa Turkiyya*
plain coffee	*gahwa saada*
sweet coffee	*gahwa ḥilwa*
ice cream	doondirma
juice	⁹asiir
milk	ḥaliib
tea	chaay
mint tea	*chaay ni⁹naa⁹*
water	mayy
yogurt	liban

Spices, Legumes, and Grains (bhaaraat wa ḥubuub)

barley	shi⁹iir
bread (flat)	khubuz
bread (Italian loaf)	sammuun
chickpeas	hummuṣ, lablabi
cinnamon	daarsiin
clove	qrinfil
cumin	kammuun
fava beans	baajilla
flour	ṭiḥiin
ginger	skanjabiil
hot pepper	filfil ḥaar
lentil	⁹adas
oil	zeit, dihin

olive oil	zeit zytuun
pasta	ma⁹karoona
pickles	turshi
rice	timman, ruzz
saffron	zu⁹faraan
saffron rice	*timman zu⁹faraan*
salt	milih
sesame	simsim
sugar	shakar
turmeric	kurkum
vinegar	khall
wheat	hunta

Kitchen Utensils (adwaat il-mutbakh)

bowl	kaasa, taasa
cup	kuub
fork	chatal
glass	glaass
kitchen	matbakh
knife	sichchiin
matches	shikhkhaat
plate, dish	maa⁹uun
skewer	shiish
spoon	khaashuuga
teacup	istikaan chaay
tray	siiniyya

Typical Iraqi Dishes (aklaat ⁹iraaqiyya)

The following are names of some of the most popular Iraqi dishes.

Baamya. Okra stew cooked with lamb and tomato sauce, usually served with rice. Iraq has a large variety of stews.

Baqlaawa. An assortment of pastries.

Doolma/maḥshi. A variety of vegetables (vine leaves, eggplant, tomato, cabbage, onion, pepper, zucchini, and lettuce leaves) stuffed with a mixture of rice, onion, minced meat, and herbs.

Gass/shaawirma. Alternating layers of meat or chicken grilled on an upright rotating spit and served in small pieces.

Kabaab. Grilled ground meat on a skewer.

Kubba. Meat pounded with cracked wheat and cooked in different ways—grilled, fried, baked, or stewed. Kubbat Muusil (named after the city of Musil in northern Iraq) is the most famous type of kubba.

Masguuf. Fish grilled on an open, circular fire of tamarisk wood and served with tomato, onion, and spices.

Mi⁹laag. Grilled pieces of liver or heart of lamb on a skewer.

Quuzi. A grilled whole baby lamb stuffed with rice, almonds, raisins, and spices. This dish is a special treat.

Tabsi. A dish with many variations, the most popular of which is the eggplant tabsi. Ingredients include eggplant (or squash), meat (ground or pieces), tomatoes, onions, garlic, green peppers, parsley, spices, and oil, all arranged in layers and baked in an oven.

Tikka. Grilled chunks of meat on a skewer.

Shopping

Basic Words and Phrases

bargaining	mu⁹aamala
better	ahsan
cheap	rikhiis
credit card	bitaaqat i'timaan
expensive	ghaali
jeweler	saayigh
market	suug
River Market	*Suug in-Nahar*
Safafir Market	*Suug is-Safaafiir*
Saray Market	*Suug is-Saraay*
Shorja Market	*Suug ish-Shoorja*
music	moosiiqa
place	mahall
price	si⁹ir
store, shop	dukkaan, makhzan

Bargaining (mu⁹aamala)

Generally speaking, there are no fixed prices in Iraq. Prices are inflated, so you must bargain with the seller to complete a purchase and get as close as possible to the real price of the item you wish to buy. The custom of bargaining is not meant to allow one party to take advantage of the other; rather, it's a social interaction between people. In fact, the Iraqi word for bargaining, "mu⁹aamala," means interaction.

How much is . . . ?	ibbeish haadha . . . ?
This is very expensive.	haadha ghaali hwaaya.
Give me a better price.	intiini si⁹ir ahsan.
What is the last price?	shunu aakhir si⁹ir?
Go down a little.	inzil shwayya.
I will give you . . . dinars.	antiik . . . danaaniir.
Is there one cheaper than this?	aku waahid arkhas min haadha?

Going Shopping

Where is a bakery?	wein aku khabbaaz?
bookstore?	*maktaba?*
camera shop?	*mahall kaamiraat?*
candy shop?	*makhzan halawiyyaat?*
clothing store?	*makhzan malaabis?*
jeweler?	*mahal saayigh?*
pharmacy?	*saydaliyya?*
newsstand?	*mahal jaraayid?*
record store?	*mahal sharaayit muusiiqiyya?*
tobacco store?	*makhzan jigaayir?*
Where is the Safafir Market?	wein Suug is-Safaafiir?
the Shorja Market?	*Suug ish-Shoorja?*
How can I get to the Shorja Market?	shloon aruuh il-Suug ish-Shoorja?
What time does the market open?	shwakit yfattih is-suug?
the market close?	*y⁹azzil is-suug?*
Do you have . . . ?	⁹idkum . . . ?
Do you take credit cards?	taakhudh bitaaqat i'timaan?

Can I pay with traveler's checks?	mumkin adfa⁹ b-sheikaat siyaa<u>h</u>iyya?

Books, Newspapers, and Magazines (kutub, jaraayid, wa majallaat)

One of the oldest markets in Baghdad is the Saray Market, located in the old Baghdad district along the Tigris River. Here one can buy old and new books, newspapers, magazines, maps, writing materials, and so on.

bag	chiis, kiis
book	ktaab
dictionary	qaamuus
guidebook	ktaab siyaa<u>h</u>i
magazine	majalla
map	<u>kh</u>ariita
newspaper	jariida
pen, pencil	qalam

Where is the Saray Market?	wein Suug is-Saraay?
I want to buy some books.	ariid ashtari kutub.
I want a guidebook.	ariid ktaab siyaa<u>h</u>i.
Do you have newspapers in English?	⁹idkum jaraayid bil-Ingiliizi?
I want a map of Baghdad in English.	ariid <u>Kh</u>ariitat Ba<u>gh</u>daad bil-Ingiliizi.
I want a map of Iraq in English.	ariid <u>Kh</u>ariitat il-⁹iraaq bil-Ingiliizi.

I want an English-Arabic dictionary.	ariid qaamuus Ingiliizi-⁹arabi.
Do you have cookbooks?	⁹idkum kutub ⁹al-tabukh?
I'll take these books.	ariid ashtari haadhi l-kutub.
How much?	shgadd?
Please put them in a bag.	rajaa'an khalliiha b-kiis.
Thank you.	shukran.
Good-bye.	ma⁹a s-salaama.

Jewelry, Gifts, and Souvenirs

In Baghdad, the favorite market for gold, silver, and jewelry is called the Gold Market (Suug idh-Dhab). It's one of the oldest markets in the city, located on River Street (Shaari⁹ in-Nahar), which runs along the Tigris River and is connected with the Safafir Market.

carat	qiiraat
chain	zanjiil
copper	nuhaas
earrings	taraachi
gift	hadiyya
gold	dhahab
jeweler	saayigh
jewelry	mujawharaat
leather	jilid
necklace	glaada
pin	danbuus
precious stone	hajar kariim

ring	mihbas
wedding ring	ẖalqa
silver	fuzza

Where is River Street, please?	min fazlak, wein Shaari⁹ in-Nahar?
Please take me to the Gold Market.	min fazlak, waddiini l-Suug idh-Dhahab.
I'd like to buy some gifts.	ahibb ashtari hadaaya.
jewelry.	*mujawharaat.*
How much is that gold necklace?	ibbeish glaadat idh-dhahab haadhi?
How many carats?	kam qiiraat?
How much is this silver ring?	ibbeish mihbas il-fuzza?
This is very expensive.	haadha ghaali hwaaya.
What is that stone?	shunu haadha l-hajar?
It's very beautiful.	kullish hilu.
Is that pin solid gold or gold plated?	haadha id-danbuus dhahab khaalis loo bass matli dhahab?

Handicrafts and Household Items

One of the oldest markets in Baghdad is called Suug is-Safaafiir. This market is known for its brass, copper, and tin craftsmen. Another old market, where you can buy household and other items (food, textiles, cereal crops, spices, utensils, and so forth) is called Suug ish-Shoorja. These two markets are near each other in the old district of the city, with access from Rashid Street.

blanket	battaaniyya
bowl	kaasa, taasa
brass, bronze	sifir
can	9ilba, quutiyya
canned	mu9allab
carpet	zuuliyya, bsaat
copper	nuhaas, sifir
enamel	miina
fabric	qmaash
food	akil
large, big	chibiir
long	tawiil
mirror	mraaya
plate	sahan, maa9uun
pot	jidir
pottery	fikhaar
purse	junta
short	qasiir
silk	hariir
size, measurement	qiyaas
small, little	zghayir
soap	saabuun
spices	bhaaraat
textile	nasiij
tray	siiniyya

I'd like to go to the Safafir Market.	ahibb aruuh l-Suug is-Safaafiir.
I want to buy a copper tray.	ariid ashtiri siiniyya nuhaasiyya.

I'd like to see that enameled tray.	ahibb ashuuf haadhi is-siiniyya bil-miina.
Is it old or new?	hiyya qadiima loo hadiitha?
I want an old tray.	ariid siiniyya qadiima.
How much?	ibbeish?
That is too much.	haadha hwaaya.
I'll give you . . .	antiik . . .
Do you have engraved bowls?	9indak taasaat manquusha?
How old is this bowl?	shgad 9umur haadhi it-taasa?
Do you have an older bowl?	9indak taasa aqdam?
I'd like to buy textiles.	ahibb ashtari nasiij.
Where is the Shorja Market?	wein Suug ish-Shoorja?
Do you have silk?	9indak qmaash hariir?
Give me four yards of red silk, please.	intiini arba9 yaardaat hariir ahmar, rajaa'an.
Do you have a dress?	9indak fustaan?
blouses, sweaters?	*bluuzaat?*
jackets?	*jaakeitaat?*
nightwear?	*qumsaan noom?*
shirts?	*thyaab?*
shoes?	*ah dhiya?*
skirts?	*tannuuraat?*
socks?	*jwaariib?*
suits?	*badlaat, quut?*
ties?	*arbita?*
trousers?	*pantaruunaat?*
underwear?	*malaabis daakhiliyya?*

85

Do you have this in other colors?

⁹indak haadha bi-alwaann thaanya?

What kinds of fabrics?

shunu noo⁹ li-qmaash?

cotton?

qutin?

leather?

jilid?

linen?

kittaan?

nylon?

naayloon?

silk?

hariir?

wool?

suuf?

My size is . . .

qiyaasi huwwa . . .

This is large.

haadha chibiir.

small.

zghayir.

short.

qasiir.

long.

tawiil.

Photographic Supplies

black and white film	filim aswad wa abyaz
camera	kaamira
color film	filim mulawwan
copy	nuskha
development	tibaa⁹a, tahmiiz
enlargement	takbiir
film/s	filim/aflaam
flashbulbs	lampaat flaash
glossy finish	waraq lammaa⁹
matte finish	waraq gheir lammaa⁹
photo/s	suura/suwar
photographer	musawwir

reduction	tas <u>gh</u>iir
slides	slaydaat

Where is a camera shop?	wein aku mahal taswiir?
I want color film.	ariid filim mulawwan.
black and white film.	*filim aswad wa abyaz.*
slide film.	*filim slaydaat.*
with twenty exposures.	*b-⁹ishriin suura.*
with thirty-six exposures.	*b-sitta wi-tlaathiin suura.*
Do you develop film?	titba⁹ aflaam?
How much does it cost?	shgadd ykallif?
OK, make me one copy of	zein, ariid nuskha wihda min
this film.	haadha l-filim.
I'd like to enlarge this photo.	ahibb takbiir haadhi s-suura.
I'd like to print five copies of	ahibb tabu⁹ khamis suwar
this photo.	l-haadhi is-suura.
with a glossy finish.	*b-waraq lammaa⁹.*
When will they be ready?	shwakit tikhlas?
Please, can you repair this	min fazlak, tigdar tsallih haadhi
camera?	l-kaamira?
The film is stuck inside.	il-filim inhishar jawwa.
Can you take out the film,	min fazlak, tigdar ittalli⁹
please?	il-film min il-kaamira?
Thank you very much.	shukran jaziilan.

Music and Video

cassette tape	shariit kaaseit
CDs	CDs

drum	dumbug
DVD	DVD
flute	naay
lute	9uud
music	moosiiqa
musical instrument	aala moosiiqiyya
new	hadiith, jdiid
old	qadiim
popular	sha9bi
song/s	ughniya/aghaani
tape/s	shariit/shraayit
video	vidyo
videocassette	vidyo kaaseit

Do you sell music tapes?	tbii9 shraayit moosiiqiyya?
Do you sell old Iraqi music and songs?	tbii9 moosiiqa wa aghaani 9iraaqiyya qadiima?
Do you have country songs?	9indak aghaani riifiyya?
Do you have modern Iraqi songs?	9indak aghaani 9iraaqiyya hadiitha?
Do you sell classical music?	tbii9 moosiiqa klaasiikiyya?
Do you have American music?	9indak moosiiqa Amriikiyya?
Please recommend some popular Iraqi songs.	min fazlak, ikhtaarli aghaani 9iraaqiyya sha9biyya.
I want a blank tape.	ariid shariit kaaseit faarigh.
Thank you.	shukran.
Good-bye.	ma9a s-salaama.

Electrical Appliances (mu⁹iddaat kahrabaa'iyya)

adapter	muhawwila
battery	baatri
electric	kahrabaa'i
electric shaver	makinat hilaaqa kahrabaa'iyya
electrical cord	silk kahrabaa'i
electricity	kahrabaa'
electronic	ilakatrooni
hair dryer	mujaffifat sha⁹ar
radio	raadyo
tape recorder	musajjil

I want to buy a tape recorder, please.	min fazlak, ariid ashtiri musajjil.
Not an expensive one.	muu ghaali.
Do you have a cheaper one?	⁹indak waahid arkhas?
Do you sell electrical adapters?	tbii⁹ muhawwil kaharabaa'i?
Thank you.	shukran.
Good-bye.	ma⁹a s-salaama.

Personal Care and Services

Laundry and Dry Cleaning (ghasil wa kawi)

blouse, sweater	bluuz
button	dugma
cleaning	tanziif
clothes	malaabis
coat	qabbuut

dirt	wisakh
dress	fustaan, nafnuuf
dry	jaaf
dry cleaning	tanziif jaaf
gloves	chfuuf
hanger	ti⁹laaga
hole	zuruf
jacket	jaakeit
nightwear	qamiis noom
pajamas	pajaama
press	kawi
shirt	thoob
skirt	tannuura
socks	jwaariib
spot	buq⁹a, tug⁹a
suit	badla, qaat
ties	rabtaat
trousers	pantaruun
underwear	malaabis daakhiliyya
wash	ghasil

Where is a dry cleaner?	wein aku mahal li-tanziif wa kawi l-malaabis?
Can you please clean these clothes?	min fazlak, tigdar tnazzufli haadhi il-malaabis?
Cleaned and pressed.	tanziif jaaf wa kawi.
Can you please clean this jacket?	min fazlak, tigdar tnazzufli haadhi l-jaakeit?
these pajamas?	*haadhi l-pajaama?*
this shirt?	*haadha l-thoob?*

this skirt?	*haadhi t-tannuura?*
this sweater?	*haadha l-bluuz?*
these trousers?	*haadha l-pantaruun?*
I need them quickly.	mihtaajha b-sur⁹a.
When will they be done?	shwakit tkhallisha?
I need them tomorrow.	ariidha baachir.
I need them the day after tomorrow.	ariidha ⁹ugub baachir.
next week.	*l-usbuu⁹ il-jaay.*
There is a missing button.	aku dugma naagsa.
Can you sew it now?	tigdar tkhayyitha hissa?
Can you fix this hole?	tigdar tsallihli haadha iz-zuruf?
This one is still dirty.	haadha ba⁹adda wasikh.
Can you clean this spot?	tigdar tnazzuf haadhi l-buq⁹a?
Please give me some hangers.	min fazlak, intiini kam ti⁹laaga.
These are not my clothes.	haadhi muu malaabsi.
How much is the bill?	shgadd li-hsaab?
Take the money, please.	tfazzal li-fluus.
Good-bye.	ma⁹a s-salaama.

Watch Shop (saa⁹aati)

alarm clock	saa⁹at tanbiih
battery	baatri
broken (watch)	kharbaana, maksuura
hour	saa⁹a
minute	daqiiqa
repair	tasliih
second	thaaniya
table clock	saa⁹at meiz

wall clock	saa⁹at ḥaayit
watch	saa⁹a
hand (minute hand and	⁹aqrab
second hand)	
pocket watch	*saa⁹at jeib*
wristwatch	*saa⁹at iid*

Can you fix this watch for me?	tigdar tsalliḥli haadhi is-saa⁹a?
It's broken.	hiyya kharbaana.
It's running late.	hiyya takhkhir.
It's running fast.	hiyya tqaddim.
It has a broken crystal.	ij-jaama maksuura.
When will it be ready?	shwakit tikhlas?
I need it quickly.	miḥtaajha b-sur⁹a.
Do you have batteries?	⁹indak baatriyyaat?
camera batteries?	*baatriyyaat kaamira?*
good watches?	*saa⁹aat zeina?*
Swiss watches?	*saa⁹aat Swiisriyya?*
Are they expensive or	hiyya ghaalya loo muu ghaalya?
inexpensive?	
Do you have less expensive	⁹indak saa⁹aat arkhas?
watches?	
Please give me a receipt.	min faẓlak, intiini waṣil.
Thank you.	shukran.

Shoemaker (qundarchi)

black	aswad
boot	juzma
brown	joozi, asmar

brush	fircha
red	ahmar
sandal	na⁹aal
shoe	qundara, hidhaa'
shoe polish	subugh qanaadir
shoemaker	qundarchi
slipper	na⁹aal
white	abyaz

Can you fix these shoes?	tigdar tsallih haadhi l-qundara?
It has a hole.	biiha zuruf.
Shine it too.	usbughha ayzan.
Do you have shoe brushes?	⁹indak firach qanaadir?
Do you have shoe polish?	⁹indak subugh qanaadir?
When will they be ready?	shwakit tikhlas?
Can you repair them now?	tigdar tkhallisha hissa?

Barber/Hairdresser (hallaaq)

Barbers and hairdressers are generally open daily from 9:00 A.M. until 8:00 P.M., except on Monday.

back	wara
barber	hallaaq, mzayyin
beard	lihya
front	giddaam, amaam
hair	sha⁹ar
haircut	zyaan
head	raas
long	tawiil

much	hwaaya
mustache	shwaarub
neck	rugba
scissors	mugass
short	qasiir
tip	bakhshiish
top	foog, ⁹ala

Do you know a good barber?	tu⁹ruf hallaaq zein?
I'd like to make an appointment for a haircut.	ahibb asawwi maw⁹id zyaan.
Can you make it earlier?	mumkin maw⁹id asra⁹?
Can I come after five o'clock?	mumkin aji ba⁹d is-saa⁹a khamsa?
I am leaving town.	aani rah-asaafir.
Please cut my hair short in the back.	rajaa'an sawwi sha⁹ri qasiir min wara.
You can cut more.	tigdar tguss akthar.
I want my hair short.	ariid sha⁹ri qasiir.
Don't cut it too short.	la-tguss sha⁹ri hwaaya.
That is enough.	haadha kaafi.
A little more in the front.	shwayya akthar min giddaam.
A little more from the top.	shwayya akthar min foog.
That is fine, thanks.	haadha zein, shukran.
I want to dye my hair.	ariid asbug sha⁹ri.
Do you have a good shampoo?	⁹idkum shampoo zein?
How much is it?	shgadd li-hsaab?
Please take the money.	tfazzal il-ujra.
Good-bye.	ma⁹a s-salaama.

Sightseeing

At the Tourist Information Office (Maktab il-Isti⁹laamaat is-Siyaahiyya)

Where is the tourist office?	wein il-maktab is-siyaahi?
We are here for a day.	ihna hnaa yoom waahid.
We'd like to see the city landmarks.	nhibb nshuuf il-ma⁹aalim is-siyaahiyya bil-madiina.
How much is it?	shgadd is-si⁹ir?
per day?	*bil-yoom?*
per hour?	*bis-saa⁹a?*
Are there boat trips?	aku rihlaat bil-qaarib?
Are there trips to . . . ?	aku rihlaat ilaa . . . ?
Do you have information about . . . ?	⁹idkum ma⁹luumaat ⁹an . . . ?
We'd like a guide.	nhibb nista'jir daliil.
When does the tour begin?	shwakit tibda' ij-jawla?
How long is the tour?	shgadd tuul ij-jawla?
Where does it begin?	min wein tibda'?
We want to see the Abbasid Palace.	nriid nshuuf il-Qasr il-⁹abbaasi.
Baghdad University.	*Jaami⁹at Baghdaad.*
Caliphs' Mosque.	*Jaami⁹ il-Khulafaa'.*
a church.	*kaniisa.*
downtown.	*markaz il-madiina.*
the Iraqi Museum.	*il-Mathaf il-⁹iraaqi.*
Khan Mirjan.	*Khaan Mirjaan.*
the main square.	*is-saaha ir-ra'iisiyya.*
a mosque.	*jaami⁹.*

Murjaniya School.	*Madrasat il-Murjaaniyya.*
Mustansiriya School.	*Madrasat il-Mustansiriyya.*
old Baghdad.	*Baghdaad il-qadiima.*
old markets.	*l-aswaaq il-qadiima.*
a palace.	*qasir.*
Tahrir Square.	*Saahat it-Tahriir.*
The Tomb of the Unknown Soldier.	*il-Jundi il-Majhuul.*
Wastani Gate.	*Baab il-Wastaani.*
Do you have tours to Agargouf (ancient)?	⁹idkum rihlaat ilaa Agarguuf?
Babylon (ancient)?	*Baabil?*
Ctesiphon (ancient)?	*Taysafuun?, Taaq Kisra?*

Visiting Museums (ziyaarat il-mataahif)

In Iraq, and especially in Baghdad, there is a large number of magnificent museums displaying valuable antiquities, interesting modern art, and folkloric exhibits. Generally, museums are excellent; many are free or have nominal fees. Most are closed on Friday.

Where is the Iraqi Museum?	wein il-Mathaf il-⁹iraaqi?
the ticket window?	*shubbaak it-tadhaakir?*
One ticket, please.	rajaa'an, tadhkarat dikhuul.
How much is the ticket?	shgadd it-tadhkara?
Is the museum open?	il-mathaf maftuuh?
What time does it open?	ibbeish is-saa⁹a yiftah?
What time does it close?	ibbeish is-saa⁹a yughluq?

Is the museum open on Friday?	hal il-mathaf faatih yoom ij-jum⁹a?
Do you have a map for the museum?	⁹idkum khariita lil-mathaf?
Do you have a guidebook in English?	⁹idkum daliil bil-Ingiliizi?
How much are these postcards?	ibbeish il-postcartaat?
Is it OK to take pictures?	mumkin asawir?
Without using a flash.	biduun isti⁹maal flaash.
Where is the museum library?	wein maktabat il-mathaf?
Is there a cafeteria?	aku kaaftiirya?
Where is the bathroom?	wein il-hammaam?
Do you sell souvenirs here?	tbii⁹uun tuhafiyyaat hnaa?
Is this an original or a replica?	haadha asli loo taqliid?
Whose statue is this?	ilman haadha l-timthaal?
Do you have books on the epic of Gilgamesh?	⁹idkum kutub ⁹an malhamat Gilgaamish?
Thank you.	shukran.

Trip to Babylon (safra l-Baabil)

Babylon, the capital of ancient civilization, is only 90 kilometers (56 miles) south of Baghdad and 10 kilometers (6 miles) north of Hilla. This magnificent city reached its peak during the reign of King Nebuchadnezzar (605–563 B.C.), who built the Hanging Gardens, one of the Seven Wonders of the Ancient World, for his beloved wife.

I'd like to visit the city of Babylon.	ahibb azuur madiinat Baabil.
How can I go there by bus?	shloon agdar aruuhilha bil-paas?
by taxi?	*bit-taksi?*
by train?	*bil-qitaar?*
Where is the bus station to Babylon?	wein mawqif il-paas il-Baabil?
Where is the road to Babylon?	wein it-tariiq il-Baabil?
Where is the information office, please?	min fazlak, wein maktab l-isti⁹laamaat?
I'd like to visit the ruins.	ahibb azuur aathaar il-madiina.
Do you have a map for the city?	⁹idkum khariita lil-madiina?
Do you provide a tour guide for the city?	⁹idkum daliil siyaahi lil-madiina?
How much is the guide fee?	shgadd ujrat id-daliil?
How long is the tour?	shgadd muddat ij-jawla?
How much is the tour?	shgada ujrat ij-jawla?
Where are the Hanging Gardens?	wein ij-Janaa'in il-Mu⁹allaqa?
is the Ishtar Gate?	*Bawwaabat ⁹ishtaar?*
is the Lion of Babylon?	*Asad Baabil?*
is Nebuchadnezzar's Palace?	*Qasir Nabukhadnassar?*
is Procession Street?	*Shaari⁹ il-Mawkib?*
is the Tower of Babylon?	*Burij Baabil?*
How old are these ruins?	shgadd ⁹umur haadhi il-aathaar?
Where is the Euphrates River?	wein Nahar il-Furaat?
Can we go to see the river?	mumkin nruuh nshuuf in-nahar?
Babylon was a great city.	Baabil chaanat madiina ⁹aziima.
Can I buy some water?	mumkin ashtiri mayy?

How can I get to the road to (the city of) Hilla?	shloon aruuh lit-tariiq ilaa madiinat il-Hilla?
Thank you very much.	shukran jaziilan.
Good-bye.	ma⁹a s-salaama.

Visiting Mosques (ziyaarat jaami⁹)

Baghdad and other major cities in Iraq have many magnificent old and modern mosques, holy shrines, and churches. You should never go into a mosque in Iraq by yourself unless you are invited or a native accompanies you. You must, of course, be dressed properly and show respect. Women must cover their heads. The following are names of some mosques and shrines.

Al-Imam Al-Adham Mosque. The tomb of Sunni Imam Abu Hanifa, built in 1066. Located in the district of Adhamiya.

The Armenian Orthodox Church (Virgin Mary Church). One of the oldest churches in Baghdad. Located in Midan Square on Rashid Street.

The Caliphs' Mosque. Built between 902 and 1289. Across from Shorja Market on Khulafaa Street.

Kadhimain Holy Shrine. The tombs of two Shiite Imams, built in 1515. Located in the district of il-Kadhimiya.

Sheikh Abdul Kadir al-Gailani Mosque. Tomb of Sheikh Abdul Kadir al-Gailani, built after his death in 1165.

Sitt Zumurrud Khatun's Tomb (Sitt Zubeida's Tomb). Built in 1202 in Sheikh Ma'ruf district.

Where is the Caliphs' Mosque?	wein Jaami⁹ il-Khulafaa'?
Which mosque is this?	ay jaami⁹ haadha?
May I enter the mosque?	mumkin adkhul ij-jaami⁹?
Must I take my shoes off?	laazim anza⁹ hidhaa'i?
Must I cover my head?	laazim aghatti raasi?
I'd like to contribute money.	ahibb atbarra⁹ fluus.
Is this an old or a new mosque?	haadha jaami⁹ qadiim loo hadiith?
When was the mosque built?	shwakit imbina ij-jaami⁹?
What is the writing on the walls?	shunu haadhi l-kitaaba ⁹al-judraan?
May I go up the minaret?	mumkin as⁹ad il-manaara?
It's a nice view from the top of the minaret.	manzar jamiil min ⁹ala l-manaara.
What is that building?	shunu hadhiich il-binaaya?
What is the name of that bridge?	shunu isim hadhaak ij-jisir?
I'd like to see that building.	ahibb ashuuf hadhiich il-binaaya.
Can you take me to that building?	mumkin taakhudhni l-hadhiich il-binaaya?
Thank you.	shukran.

At the Tourist Village of Habbaniya Lake

A large tourist village built around the Lake of Habbaniya (Buhayrat il-Habbaaniyya) is located about 84 kilometers (52 miles) west of Baghdad. The village includes a hotel, restaurants, swimming pools, sailboats, a riding stable, sports facilities, a market, a casino, a cinema, and children's playgrounds. It is a place for relaxation and enjoyment.

Where is Habbaniya Lake?	wein Buhayrat il-Habbaaniyya?
I heard it was very nice.	sima⁹it hiyya hilwa hwaaya.
It's not far from Baghdad.	hiyya muu bi⁹iida min Baghdaad.
Can I get there by bus?	agdar aruuhilha bil-paas?
by taxi?	*bil-taksi?*
Which bus shall I take?	ay paas laazim aakhudh?
Must I make a reservation before I go?	laazim asawwi hajiz gabul ma-aruuh?
Please reserve one bedroom with two beds for me.	rajaa'an, ihjizli ghurfa b-sariirein.
for two nights.	*leiltein.*
I want to rent a boat.	ariid ta'jiir balam.
a cabin.	*kaabiina.*
a sailboat.	*balam shiraa⁹i.*
scuba equipment.	*mu⁹iddaat ghatis.*
a tennis racket.	*rikit maal tanis.*
an umbrella.	*mazalla shamsiyya.*
Do you have a swimming pool for children?	⁹idkum masbah lil-atfaal?
Are there any showers?	wein aku duushaat?
Can I fish here?	agdar asiid simach hnaa?
Is it OK to swim here?	maykhaalif asbah hnaa?

Entertainment

Basic Words and Phrases

art	fann
bar	baar
casino	gaaziino
cinema	siinama
club	naadi
nightclub	*malha, naadi leili*
social club	*naadi ijtimaa⁹i*
sports club	*naadi riyaazi*
coffee shop	gahwa
concert	hafla moosiiqiyya
dance	rigis
exhibit	ma⁹raz
art exhibit	*ma⁹raz fanni*
lake	buhayra
movie, film	filim
music	moosiiqa
Eastern music	*moosiiqa sharqiyya*
music concert	*hafla moosiiqiyya*
Western music	*moosiiqa gharbiyya*
play	masrahiyya
show	⁹ariz
theater	masrah
ticket	tadhkara, tikit
ticket window	shubbaak it-tadhaakir

At the Ticket Window (⁹ind shubbaak it-tadhaakir)

I'd like two tickets for the art exhibit.	ahibb tiktein lil-ma⁹raz il-fanni.
the music concert.	*lil-hafla il-moosiiqiyya.*
the play.	*lil-masrahiyya.*
tonight's movie.	*li-filim il-leila.*
How much are the tickets?	shgadd it-tadhaakir?
Are there less expensive tickets?	aku tadhaakir arkhas?
I'd like to make a reservation for Friday.	ahibb ahjiz l-yoom ij-jum⁹a.
What time does the show start?	ay waqit yibdi il-⁹ariz?
May I have a program, please?	ariid barnaamij, min fazlak.
Thank you.	shukran.

At the Cinema (bis-siinama)

Let's go to the cinema.	khalliina nruuh lis-siinama.
Which cinema?	ay siinama?
On Sadoun Street.	b-Shaari⁹ is-Sa⁹duun.
What kind of movie is it?	shunu noo⁹ il-filim?
Is it an American movie?	il-filim Amriiki?
Is it in Arabic or English?	il-filim bi-lugha l-⁹arabiyya loo l-Ingiliiziyya?
Is the movie dubbed or subtitled?	il-filim mudablaj loo mutarjam?
What time does the film start?	shwakit yibdi il-filim?
I'd like some juice, please.	min fazlak, ahibb ⁹asiir.
Where is the toilet, please?	min fazlak, wein li-twaaleit?
Thank you.	shukran.

103

At the Theater/Concert (bil-masrah)

Where is the National Theatre?	wein il-Masrah il-Watani?
What is playing tonight?	ayy masrahiyya il-leila?
Is it a local or an international group?	il-firqa mahalliyya loo ⁹aalamiyya?
What is the name of the play?	shunu isim il-masrahiyya?
I'd like one ticket to the folk dance.	ariid tadhkara lir-riqs ish-sha⁹bi.
the music concert.	*lil-hafla ilmoosiiqiyya.*
tonight's opera.	*l-masrahiyat il-leila.*
I don't want expensive tickets.	ma-ariid tadhkara ghaalya.
Who is the singer?	minu il-mughanni?
Who is the dancer?	minu ir-raaqisa?
Is a group dancing?	hiyya firqa raaqisa?
Is it Arabic or European music?	il-moosiiqa ⁹arabiyya loo Awruppiyya?
Is the group popular?	il-firqa mashhuura?
I like Arabic music.	aani ahibb il-moosiiqa l-⁹arabiyya.

At the Nightclub (bil-malha)

Let's go to a nightclub.	khalliina nruuh lil-malha.
Where is a very good nightclub?	wein aku malha kullish zein?
Is the nightclub Nojoum good?	malha Nojoum zein?
What kind of music do they play?	ay noo⁹ moosiiqa y⁹izfuun?
Eastern and Western music with dancing.	moosiiqa sharqiyya wa gharbiyya wiyya rigis.

Is evening dress required?	laazim albas malaabis sahra?
Must we make a reservation?	laazim nihjiz?
Is food served in the nightclub?	yuqaadam it-ta⁹aam bil-malha?
Let's have an exciting night.	khalliina nis-har leila muthiira.
Call us a taxi.	khaaburinna ⁹ala taksi.
Is there music and dancing in the hotel?	aku riqis w moosiiqa bil-findiq?
Reserve us a nice table, please.	min fazlak, ihjizinna meiz zein.
What time does the show start?	shwakit yibdi il-⁹arz?

At the Social/Sports Club (b-naadi ijtimaa⁹i/riyaazi)

There are several social clubs (also called sports clubs) in the major cities of Iraq. To attend a club, you must be a member or the guest of a member. Here you can find many European/American amenities—sports activities (such as swimming and tennis), parties, films, dancing, and good food and drink.

Are there social clubs in Baghdad?	aku nawaadi ijtimaa⁹iyya b-Baghdaad?
How can I go to one of them?	shloon agdar aruuh il-waahid minha?
Are you a member of a club?	inta ⁹uzu b-naadi?
Can I go with you sometime?	mumkin aruuh wiyyaak fad marra?
Can I become a member?	agdar asiir ⁹uzu?
I'd very much like to swim.	ahibb asbah hwaaya.
play tennis.	*al⁹ab tanis.*

I'd like to see a racetrack.

What sport do you like?

I like basketball.

> *boxing.*
>
> *jogging.*
>
> *soccer.*
>
> *swimming.*
>
> *tennis.*
>
> *walking.*

Thank you very much.

ahibb ashuuf sibaaq kheil.

ay riyaaza thibb?

ahibb kurat is-salla.

> *mulaakama.*
>
> *harwala.*
>
> *kurat il-qadam.*
>
> *sibaaha.*
>
> *tanis.*
>
> *il-mishi.*

shukran jaziilan.

Chapter 4

Specialized Phrases

Idioms and Common Phrases

As you wish.	iddallal.
At your service.	b-khidimtak.
Be careful.	diir baalak.
By the way, . . .	⁹ala fikra, . . .
definitely, really	walla
[Someone] doesn't care what happens.	dhaabha ⁹as-saatuur.
Don't worry about tomorrow.	mminu abu baachir.
Enjoy (your food/drink).	bil-⁹aafya.
from now on	min hissa w-jaay
God willing	ˉinshaalla
Good for you.	⁹afya ⁹aleik.
good person	ibn awaadim
[Someone] has no shame!	ma-yistihi!
How do you know?	shmadriik?
Hurry up!	yalla!

I'll pay.	⁹ala ḥsaabi., ⁹alayya.
I'm upset.	zahgaan., ruuḥi taal⁹a.
Is it up for grabs?	qaabil farhuud?
It can't be., Impossible.	maysiir.
It's good to see you.	⁹aash min shaafak.
It's not my fault., It's not in my hands.	aani sha ⁹layya.
It's OK.	maashi l-ḥaal.
Leave it to God.	khalliiha ⁹alalla.
Luck is needed.	yinraadilha ḥazz.
neither expensive nor cheap	laa ghaali wala rkhiis
no need for	maaku luzuum
No way!	maa mumkin!
not bad	laa shiish wala kabaab
nowadays	hal-ayyaam
of course	tab⁹an
please, if you don't mind	bduun zaḥma
Shame on you!	⁹eib ⁹aleik!
so, in that case	la⁹ad
still too early to leave	ba⁹ad wakit
Take it easy!	⁹ala keifak!
thankful, grateful	mamnuun
This is easy (to do).	haay basiita.
What did you think?	sh⁹abaalak?
whatever you give me	alla w-iidak
What's going on?	haay shaku?
What's up?, What's new?	shaku maaku?
Where have you been?	haay ween inta?
with pleasure	⁹ala ⁹eini, ⁹ala raasi

| You don't say! | laa balla! |
| You were missed. | mukaanak khaali. |

Countries and Nationalities

Basic Words and Phrases

Africa	Afriiqya
America	Amriika
Asia	Aasya
continent	qaara
country	balad/qutur
Europe	Awrupaa
gulf	khaliij
island	jaziira
Middle East (the)	ish-Sharq il-Awsat
nation	watan
nationalist	watani
nationality	jinsiyya
ocean	muhiit
sea	bahar

Arab and Islamic Countries

	Country	**Nationality**
Algeria	il-Jazaa'ir	Jazaa'iri
Afghanistan	Afghaanistaan	Afghaanistaani
Bahrain	il-Bahrein	Bahreini
Egypt	Masir	Masri

Indonesia	Anduunosya	Anduunosi
Iran	Iraan	Iraani
Iraq	il-⁹iraaq	⁹iraaqi
Kuwait	il-Kuweit	Kuweiti
Lebanon	Lubnaan	Lubnaani
Libya	Liibya	Liibi
Morocco	il-Maghrib	Maghribi
Oman	⁹umaan	⁹umaani
Pakistan	Paakistaan	Paakistaani
Palestine	Filistiin	Filistiini
Qatar	Qatar	Qatari
Saudi Arabia	is-Su⁹uudiyya	Su⁹uudi
Somalia	is-Suumaal	Suumaali
Sudan	il-Suudaan	Suudaani
Syria	Suurya	Suuri
Tunisia	Tuunis	Tuunisi
Turkey	Turkiya	Turki
United Arab Emirates	il-Imaaraat il-⁹arabiyya il-Muttahida	Imaaraati
Yemen	il-Yaman	Yamani

Asian, Australian, and European Countries

	Country	Nationality
Australia	Istiraaliya	Istiraali
China	is-Siin	Siini
Denmark	id-Daaniimark	Daniimarki
England	Ingiltara	Ingiliizi

France	Fransa	Fransi
Germany	Almaanya	Almaani
Great Britain	Bariitanya	Bariitaani
Greece	il-Yuunaan	Yuunaani
Holland	Hoolanda	Hoolandi
India	il-Hind	Hindi
Ireland	Irlanda	Irlandi
Italy	Itaalya	Itaali
Japan	il-Yaabaan	Yaabaani
Korea	Koorya	Koori
Poland	Poolanda	Poolandi
Portugal	il-Purtughaal	Purtughaali
Russia	Ruusya	Ruusi
Spain	Ispaanya	Ispaani
Sweden	is-Suwiid	Suwiidi
Switzerland	Swiisra	Swiisri
Vietnam	Fiitnaam	Fiitnaami

American and African Countries

	Country	Nationality
America	Amriika	Amriiki
Angola	Anguula	Anguuli
Argentina	il-Arjantiin	Arjantiini
Brazil	il-Baraaziil	Baraaziili
Canada	Kanada	Kanadi
Chile	Shiili	Shiili
Ethiopia	Ithyoobya	Ithyoobi
Kenya	Kiinya	Kiini

Mexico	il-Maksiik	Maksiiki
South Africa	Afriiqya ij-Junuubiya	Afriiqi Junuubi
Uganda	Yoo<u>g</u>handa	Yoo<u>g</u>handi

I am from France.	aani min Fransa.
I am French.	aani Fransi.
You (*f.*) are from Britain.	inti min Briitaanya.
You (*f.*) are British.	inti Briitaaniyya.
Where is Italy?	wein Itaalya?
It's in Europe.	hiyya fii Awruppa.
Are you an American or a European?	inta Amriiki loo Awruppi?

Archaeology and Museums

Modern Iraq, which encompasses ancient Mesopotamia, is the cradle of Western civilization. It's the land of Sumer, Babylonia, and Assyria, which gave birth to most of the elements of our present civilizations. This is the country of great ancient cities like Ur, Babylon, Nineveh, and Baghdad. Travelers in this country can't fail to notice and appreciate the surroundings of seven thousand years of history.

Basic Words and Phrases

ancient, old	qadiim, athari
archaeologist	aathaari
archaeology, antiquities	aathaar
Babylon (ancient city and land)	Baabil
city	madiina
Directorate General of Antiquities (Baghdad)	Mudiiriyat il-Aathaar il-⁹aama (Baghdaad)
Euphrates River	Nahar il-Furaat
guide	daliil
guidebook	daliil siyaahi
excavation	tanqiibaat
information office	maktab isti⁹laamaat
minaret	manaara
modern	hadiith
mosque	jaami⁹
mound	tall
museum	mathaf
new	jdiid
site	mawqi⁹

Sumer (ancient land of southern Iraq)	Soomar
ticket	tadhkara, tikit
Tigris River	Nahar Dijla
tour	jawla, rihla
ziggurat (ancient staged structure)	zaqquura

Museums in Baghdad

Baghdad Museum (Mathaf Baghdaad). Located on Mamoun Street near the Martyrs' Bridge. It houses life-size sculptures in traditional Iraqi costumes.

The Iraqi Museum (il-Mathaf il-⁹iraaqi). Located on the Museum Square in the Karch district. It contains magnificent antiquities ranging from the prehistoric era to the Islamic era.

Museum of National Costume and Folklore (Mathaf il-Fooluk-loor wil-Azyaa' il-Wataniyya). Located on Rashid Street, on the eastern bank of the Tigris River. The museum is in an original Baghdadi building.

Museum of Pioneer Artists (Mathaf il-Fanaaniin ir-Ruwwad). Located next to the Museum of National Costume and Folklore on Rashid Street. It exhibits an interesting collection of paintings by pioneer Iraqi artists in a Baghdadi-style house built in 1909.

Museum of Popular Heritage (Mathaf il-Turaath ish-Sha⁹bi). Located on Haifa Street. It contains examples of traditional Iraqi craftsmanship.

Mustansiriya School (Madrasat il-Mustansiriyya). Overlooks the Tigris River next to the Shuhada' Bridge. Built in the early thirteenth century A.D., it became the most prominent university during the Abbasid Dynasty.

National Museum of Modern Art (il-Mathaf il-Watani lil-Funuun il-Hadiitha). Located on Kifah Street. It houses Iraqi modern art in a permanent collection of paintings, sculptures, and ceramics.

The War Museum (il-Mathaf il-Harbi). Located on Adhamiya River Drive in Kasra district. It exhibits old weaponry and military equipment.

On an Archaeological Site (b-mawqi⁹ athari)

ancient mound	tall athari
archaeological expedition	bi⁹tha athariyya
archaeologist	aathaari
archaeology, antiquities	aathaar
bone	⁹azum
brick	taabuug
building	binaa'
camp	mukhayyam
clay, adobe	tiin
dig	hafur
digger	haffaar
digging equipment	adawaat hafur
ditch	hufra
excavation	hafriyyaat
excavator	munaqqib
expedition, mission	bi⁹tha
field director	mudiir bi⁹tha

foreman	usta
grave	gabur
hoe	mishaa
house	beit
metal	ma⁹dan
mound, tell	tall
mud brick	libin
objects	mawaad
period	⁹asir, fatra
pick	qazma
potsherd	kisrat fikhaar
seal	khatam
cylinder seal	*khatm istiwaani*
stone	hajar, sakhar
tablet	raqiim
temple	ma⁹bad
tent	kheima
trench	khandaq
worker	⁹aamil
writing	kitaaba
cuneiform writing	*kitaaba mismaariyya*

This is a large archaeological tell.	haadha tall athari chibiir.
What is the age of this tell?	min ay ⁹asir haadha it-tall?
The Sumerian or the Babylonian age?	il-asir il-Soomari loo il-Baabili?
Is this a house or a temple?	haadha beit loo ma⁹bad?

What period are these potsherds?	min ay ⁹asir haadhi l-kisar il-fikhaariyya?
This is a group of bones and metals.	haadhi majmuu⁹a min ⁹zamm wa ma⁹aadin.
This tablet has writing.	haadha ir-raqiim ⁹alei kitaaba.
Babylonian cuneiform	kitaaba mismaariyya Baabiliyya
May I come inside the building?	mumkin aji daakhil il-binaa'?
What is that on the floor of the room?	shunu haadha ⁹ala arziyyat il-ghurfa?
Give me a brush, please.	intiini fircha, rajaa'an.
I am making a drawing of the building.	aani arsim mukhatat lil-binaa'.
I am taking these objects to the tent.	aani aakhudh haadhi l-mawaad lil-kheima.
How many months do you dig here?	kam shahar thufruun hnaa?
Three months a year.	tlath tushhur bis-sana.
I like excavations.	aani ahibb it-tanqiibaat.

Medical Care

Basic Words and Phrases

appointment	maw⁹id
clinic	mustawsif
dentist	tabiib asnaan
diagnosis	tashkhiis
doctor, physician	tabiib, diktoor
ear, nose, and throat doctor	tabiib idhin, anff, wa hunjura

examination	faḥis
eye doctor	tabiib ⁹uyuun
gynecologist	tabiib nisaa'iyyaat
health	siḥha
hospital	mustashfa
state hospital	*mustashfa ḥukuumi*
laboratory	mukḥtabar
lab test	taḥliil
man	rajul, rijjaal
medicine	diwa
nurse	mumarriẓa
orthopedist	tabiib ⁹iẓaam
optician	⁹uweinaati, naẓẓaaraati
pain	wija⁹, alam
patient	mariiz
pharmacist	ṣaydali
pharmacy	ṣaydaliyya
pill/s	ḥabba/ḥubuub
symptoms	a⁹raaẓ
syringe	ḥuqna
toothbrush	firchat asnaan
toothpaste	ma⁹joon asnaan
treatment	⁹ilaaj
urine	bool
vitamins	fiitaamiinaat
wing (hospital)	radha
woman	mara

Names of Body Parts (asmaa' aqsaam ij-jisim)

ankle	mafsal qadam
appendix	iz-zaa'ida id-duudiyya
arm	dhiraa⁹
back	zahar
bladder	mathaana
blood	damm
body	jisim
bone	⁹azum
cheek	khadd
chest	sadir
ear	idhin
eye	⁹ein
face	wijih
finger	isbi⁹
foot	qadam
hair	sha⁹ar
hand	iid
head	raas
heart	galub
jaw	fachch
joint	mafsal
kidney	kilya
knee	rukba
leg	rijil
lip	shiffa
liver	kabad
lung	ri'a
mouth	halig

neck	rugba
nose	anff, khashim
shoulder	chitif
skin	jilid
stomach	mi⁹da
teeth	asnaan
thigh	fukhidh
throat	hunjira, zarduum
thumb	isbi⁹ ibhaam
toe	isbi⁹ (qdam)
tongue	lsaan
vein	damaar
wrist	rusugh

With the Doctor (⁹ind it-tabiib)

I don't feel well.	maa ⁹indi khulug.
I need a doctor.	ahtaaj tabiib.
It's urgent.	haala musta⁹jala.
Do you know a doctor who speaks English?	tu⁹ruf tabiib yitkallam Ingiliizi?
Where is his office?	wein maktaba?
Will the doctor come here?	mumkin it-tabiib yiji hnaa?
Let's go to the doctor.	khalliina nruuh lit-tabiib.
It hurts here.	yuja⁹ni hnaa.
My whole body hurts.	jismi kulla yuja⁹ni.
I feel weak.	ash⁹ur b-zu⁹uf.
I feel dizzy.	ash⁹ur b-dookha.
I feel sick.	ash⁹ur mariiz.

I have an allergy.	⁹indi ḥassaasiyya.
back pain.	*wija⁹ b-ẕahri.*
bleeding.	*naziif ḏamm.*
a broken bone.	*⁹azum maksuur.*
cancer.	*sarataan.*
a cold.	*nashla.*
a cough.	*gaḥḥa.*
diabetes	*sukkar.*
diarrhea.	*is-haal.*
a fever.	*ḥaraara.*
gas.	*ghaazaat.*
a headache.	*wija⁹ raas.*
a heart condition.	*ḥaala qalbiyya.*
high blood pressure.	*ẕaghit ḏamm ⁹aali.*
indigestion.	*suu' hazum.*
a pain in my stomach.	*wija⁹ b-mi⁹idti.*
poisoning.	*tasammum.*
a sore throat.	*wija⁹ bal⁹uum.*
a stiff neck.	*wija⁹ b-rugubti.*
sunburn.	*ḥargat shamis.*
a toothache.	*wija⁹ asnaan.*
This is my usual medicine.	haaḏha diwaaya il-⁹aadi.
Please give me the bill.	min faẕlak inṯiini li-ḥsaab.

Women's Health (taṯbiib nisaa'i)

Is there a gynecologist?	aku ṯabiib nisaa'iyyaat?
Is there a female doctor?	aku ṯabiiba hnaa?
I prefer a woman.	aani afaẕẕil ṯabiiba tifḥasni.

I may be pregnant.	mumkin akuun <u>h</u>aamil.
I'd like to have a pregnancy test.	a<u>h</u>ibb aa<u>kh</u>u<u>dh</u> <u>f</u>a<u>h</u>is <u>h</u>aamil.
I haven't had my period for two months.	maa jatni l-⁹aada l-shahrein.
I have abdominal pain.	⁹indi wija⁹ baatini.
I take birth control pills.	aa<u>kh</u>udh hubuub man⁹ il-hamil.
I use a diaphragm.	asta⁹mil diaphragm.

Doctor's Instructions (ta⁹liimaat it-tabiib)

Open your mouth.	ifta<u>h</u> <u>h</u>algak.
Stick out your tongue.	<u>t</u>alli⁹ lsaanak.
Cough.	gu<u>hh</u>., i⁹tis.
Take a deep breath.	u<u>kh</u>u<u>dh</u> nafas ⁹amiiq.
Take off your clothes.	inza⁹ malaabsak.
Lie down.	istalqi ⁹as-sariir.
Where does it hurt?	wein il-alam?
Stand up.	oogaf.
Get dressed.	ilbas malaabsak.

Patient Follow-Up (mutaaba⁹at il-mariiz)

Are you giving me a prescription?	ra<u>h</u>-tintiini was<u>f</u>a?
How often should I take the medicine?	kam marra bil-yoom laazim aa<u>kh</u>udh id-diwa?
How long must I stay in bed?	shgadd laazim abqa bli-fraash?

Do you want me to come back?	triidni arja⁹?
Thank you very much for your help.	shukran jaziilan ⁹ala musaa⁹attak.
Good-bye.	ma⁹a s-salaama.

In the Hospital (bil-mustashfa)

Someone help me!	waahid ysaa⁹idni!
Call a doctor quickly!	siih tabiib b-sur⁹a!
Call an ambulance!	siih sayyaarat is⁹aaf!
It's an emergency!	haala mista⁹jila!
Take him to the hospital!	waddii lil-mustashfa!
I fell down.	wga⁹it.
Somebody hit me.	waahid zirabni.
A car hit me.	sayyaara zirbatni.
I cut myself.	jrahit nafsi.
I burned myself.	ihtiragit.
I am bleeding.	⁹indi naziif.
I have a broken bone.	⁹indi ⁹azum maksuur.
I twisted/sprained my ankle.	lweit mafsali.
arm.	*dhiraa⁹i.*
back.	*zahri.*
knee.	*rukubti.*
leg.	*rijli.*
wrist.	*mi⁹sami.*
My arm is swollen.	dhiraa⁹i waarma.
I can't move my leg.	maa agdar aharrik rijli.
my neck.	*rugubti.*
When will the doctor come?	shwakit yiji it-tabiib?

I can't eat.	maa agdar aakul.
I can't sleep.	maa agdar anaam.
What is the name of this hospital?	shunu isim haadhi il-mustashfa?
Please notify my family.	rajaa'an khaaburu ahli.
Please notify my embassy.	rajaa'an khaaburu safaarti.
Which wing is he in?	huwwa fii ayy radha?
I am visiting . . .	aani azuur . . .
Thank you.	shukran.

At the Dentist ('ind tabiib l-asnaan)

Do you know a good dentist?	tu⁹ruf tabiib asnaan zein?
I have a toothache.	⁹indi alam asnaan.
In this tooth.	b-haadha is-sinn.
I've lost a filling.	wig⁹at hashwat sinni.
I have a cavity.	⁹indi tsawwis b-sinni.
My gums are swollen.	lathti miltahba.
I have an infection in my mouth.	⁹indi iltihaab b-halgi.
I have a broken tooth.	⁹indi sinn maksuur.
Don't extract it, please.	la-tikhla⁹ sinni, min fazlak.
Please give me an anesthetic.	min fazlak, intiini mukhaddir.
Can you fix this tooth?	tigdar tsallih haadha is-sinn?
this bridge?	*haadha ij-jisir?*
this crown?	*haadha it-taaj?*
Should I come back?	laazim arja⁹?
When should I come back?	shwakit lazzim arja⁹?
How much is the bill?	shgadd li-hsaab?
Thank you.	shukran.

At the Pharmacy (bis-saydaliyya)

Where is the closest pharmacy?	wein aqrab saydaliyya?
Is it open late at night?	maftuuha mitakhkhir bil-leil?
Is this medicine available?	mitwaffir haadha id-diwa?
Does it have side effects?	bii a⁹raaz jaanabiyya?
I want medicine for a cold.	ariid diwa nashla.
a cough.	*gahha.*
diarrhea.	*is-haal.*
a fever.	*haraara.*
a headache	*wija⁹ raas.*
a toothache.	*wija⁹ sinn.*
an upset stomach.	*maghas mi⁹da.*
a sore throat.	*wija⁹ bal⁹uum.*
I don't have a prescription.	maa ⁹indy wasfat tabiib.
This is the prescription.	haadhi wasfat it-tabiib.
Hurry, please!	bsur⁹a alla ykhalliik!
It's an emergency!	haala mista⁹jala!
How many shall I take each time?	kam habbaaya aakhudh kull marra?
How many times per day?	kam marra bil-yoom?
I want to buy antibiotics.	ariid ashtiri antibaayootiks.
aspirin.	*aspiriin.*
a bandage.	*zammaada.*
condoms.	*flaash ladhar.*
contraceptives.	*hubuub man⁹ il-hamil.*
cotton.	*gutun.*
cough medicine.	*diwa lil-gahha.*
eardrops.	*gatrat adhaan.*
eyedrops.	*gatrat ⁹iyuun.*

iodine.	yood.
ointment.	dihin.
pain killers.	hubuub musakkina.
powder.	poodar.
sleeping pills.	hubuub munawwima.
soap.	saabuun.
sunglasses.	nazzaaraat shamsiyya.
tape.	shariit lazig.
tissue paper.	kliinaks.
a toothbrush.	firchat asnaan.
toothpaste.	ma⁹joon asnaan.
vitamins.	vitaamiinaat.

At the Optometrist (⁹ind tabiib li-ʾyuun)

I am farsighted.	⁹indi bu⁹ud nazar.
I am nearsighted.	⁹indi qusur nazar.
I have lost my contact lenses.	zayya⁹it ⁹adasaati il-laasiqa.
Can you replace them quickly?	tigdar tbaddilha b-sur⁹a?
I have lost my reading glasses.	zayya'it nazzaaraati lil-qiraa'a.
Can you repair my glasses?	tigdar tsallih manaazri?
Can you tighten the screws?	tigdar izzub il-baraaghi?
Can you replace the lens?	tigdar tbaddil iz-zujaaj?
Can you make me new glasses?	tigdar tsawwiili nazzaaraat jdiida?
I'd like contact lense solution.	ariid mahluul ⁹adasaat laasiqa.
Can you test my eyes?	tigdar tifhas ⁹yuuni?
Thank you.	shukran.

Media

Basic Words and Phrases

broadcaster	mudhii⁹
director	mudiir
employee, official	muwazzaf
government official	muwazzaf hukuumi
journalist	sahafi
journalistic report, news story	taqriir sahafi
magazine	majalla
media	i⁹laam
news	akhbaar
international news	*akhbaar ⁹aalamiyya*
local news	*akhbaar mahalliyya*
news bulletin	nashrat akhbaar
newspaper	jariida, sahiifa
occupation	shughul, waziifa
program	barnaamij
radio	raadyo
radio station	idhaa⁹a
reporter	muraasil
station	mahatta
thankful, indebted	mamnuun
TV	talfizyoon
TV station	mahatta talfizyooniyya

What is your occupation?	shunu shughlak?
I am a journalist with *Time* magazine.	aani sahafi wiyya Majalat al-Taaymz.

I am a reporter with the *Tribune*.	aani muraasil wiyya S̲ahiifat al-Tribyuun.
I am a broadcaster with the PBC.	aani mud̲hii⁹ fii Idhaa⁹at PBC.
I am writing a news story.	aani da-aktib taqriir s̲ahafi.
May I ask you some questions?	mumkin as'alak kam su'aal?
Can you help me arrange an appointment?	tigdar tsaa⁹idni fii tanziim muqaabala?
with the director of the TV station?	*wiyya mudiir mah̲att̲at it-talfizyoon?*
tomorrow.	*baachir.*
the day after tomorrow.	*⁹ugub baachir.*
I would be grateful.	akuun mamnuunlak.
How many news bulletins do you have per day?	kam nashra akh̲baar ⁹idkum bil-yoom?
Do you have news in English?	⁹idkum nashra bil-lug̲ha l-Ingiliiziyya?
At what time?	shwakit?
Do you have a translation division?	⁹idkum qisim tarjama?
Thank you very much.	shukran jaziilan.
Good-bye.	ma⁹a s-salaama.

Lost or Stolen

Basic Words and Phrases

airline ticket	tad̲hkirat t̲ayyaara
camera	kaamira

credit card	butaaqat i'timaan
daughter	bint
driver's license	ijaazat siyaaqa
handbag	juntat iid
husband	zooj
insurance company	sharikat ta'miin
jewelry	mujawharaat
key	miftaah
car key	*miftaah is-sayyaara*
lost	mafquud, zaayi⁹
money	fluus
passport	paasporti, jwaaz safar
police	shurta, pooliis
police station	markaz shurta
son	ibin
stolen	masruuq, mabyuug
wallet	jizdaan
watch	saa⁹a
wife	zooja

At the Police Station (b-markaz shurta)

Where is the closest police station?	wein aqrab markaz shurta?
Is there somebody who speaks English?	aku waahid yitkallam Ingiliizi?
My son is lost.	zaa⁹ ibni.
My daughter is lost.	zaa⁹at binti.
My wife is lost.	zaa⁹at zoojti.

129

My husband is lost.	z̲aa⁹ zooji.
This is his picture.	haad̲hi suurta.
This is her picture.	haad̲hi suurat-ha.
He has blond hair.	sha⁹ra ashgar.
He has blue eyes.	⁹yuuna zurug.
He is tall.	huwwa tawiil.
He is short.	huwwa qas̲iir.
He is ten years old.	⁹umra ⁹ashr sniin.
He disappeared six hours ago.	ikhtifa gabul sit saa⁹aat.
Can I use the telephone?	agdar asta⁹mil it-talafoon?
I need to contact the German embassy.	ariid attasil bis-safaara il-Almaaniyya.
Thank you for your help.	shukran ⁹ala musaa⁹attak.

Theft (sariqa)

Somebody has stolen my camera.	waah̲id baag kaamirti.
my handbag.	*junutti.*
my money.	*fluusi.*
my wallet.	*jisdaani.*
my watch.	*saa⁹ti.*
Someone broke into my car.	waah̲id kisar sayyaarti.
and stole my passport.	*wa baag paasporti.*
I need a police report for my insurance company.	ariid taqriir shurt̲a li-sharikat it-ta'miin maalti.
Thank you very much.	shukran jaziilan.

Lost (zaayi⁹)

I have lost my airline ticket.	zayya⁹it tadhkirat tayyaarti.
car key.	*miftaah sayyaarti.*
credit card.	*butaaqat i'timaani.*
driving license.	*rukhsat is-siyaaqa.*
jewelry.	*jawaahiri.*
passport.	*paasporti.*
They were in the car.	kaanat bis-sayyaara.
They were in my room.	kaanat b-ghurufti.
What should I do?	sh-sawwi?
Should I go to the police?	aruuh lish-shurta?

Security and Visa (amin wa viiza)

Basic Words and Phrases

agency	wakaala, hay'a
army	jaysh
border	huduud
border crossing	ma⁹bar huduud
checkpoint, searchpoint	nuqtat taftiish
Department of Travel and Naturalization	Mudiiriyyat is-Safar wij-Jinsiyya
employee	muwazzaf
military	⁹askari
ministry	wizaara
Ministry of Defense	Wizaarat id-Difaa⁹
officer	zaabut
order	amur

police	shurta
traffic police	*shurtat muruur*
police station	markaz shurta
prison	sijin
Resident's Department	Mudiiriyyat il-Iqaama
search	taftiish
security	amin
Security General Department	Mudiiriyyat il-Amn il-⁹aamma
Stop!	oogaf!
United Nations	Munazzamat il-Umam il-Muttahida
visa	viiza
weapon/s	slaah/asliha

Getting a Visa (tahsiil viiza)

Where can I get a visa?	wein agdar ahassil viiza?
Where can I renew my visa?	wein agdar ajaddid viizti?
At the Department of Travel and Naturalization.	b-Mudiiriyyat is-Safar wij-Jinsiyya.
Do you think you can come with me?	mumkin tiji wiyyaaya?
I'd like to renew my visa, please.	min fazlak, ahibb ajaddid viizti.
It will expire in two weeks.	rah-tintihi ba⁹ad usbuu⁹ein.
I'd like to stay one more month.	ahibb abqa shahar aakhar.
I am a reporter from Canada writing a news story on Babylon.	aani muraasil min Kanada aktib taqriir sahafi ⁹an Baabil.
I have a tourist visa.	⁹indi viiza siyaahiyya.

I am visiting relatives.	aani azuur ahli.
Here is my passport.	haadha paasporti.
Here are my documents.	haadhi awraaqi.
I am staying at this hotel.	aani naazil bhal-uteil.
My address is . . .	⁹unwaani . . .
I also have my wife with me.	zoojti wiyyaaya.
but she does not need a visa.	*bass hiyya ma-tihtaaj viiza.*
How much are the fees?	shgadd ir-risum?
Thank you very much.	shukran jaziilan.
Good-bye.	ma⁹a s-salaama.

At a Checkpoint (nuqtat taftiish)

Slow down, there is a checkpoint ahead of us!	⁹ala keifak, aku nuqtat taftiish giddaamna!
Stop the car!	waggof is-sayyaara!
There are soldiers with weapons.	aku junuud musallahiin.
Let me speak with them.	khalliini atkallam wiyyaahum.
May God help you.	alla ysa⁹idkum.
How are you today?	shloonkum il-yoom?
I am an employee from the United Nations.	aani muwazzaf min Munazzamat il-Umam il-Muttahida.
I work with the humanitarian agency.	a⁹mal ma⁹a wakaalat il-Musaa⁹adaat il-Insaaniyya.
This is my official driver, Mr. Kaamil.	haadha is-saayiq ir-rasmi, sayyid Kaamil.
We are heading to the city of Hilla.	ihna raayhiin ilaa madinat il-Hilla.
This is my passport.	haadha paasporti.

These are my official papers.	haadhi awraaqi ir-rasmiyya.
Do you want to search the car?	triiduun tfatshuun is-sayyaara?
Do you want me to open the trunk?	triiduuni aftah is-sanduug?
Kaamil, open the trunk, please.	Kaamil, iftah is-sanduug, min fazlak.
Do you want anything else?	triiduun shii aakhar?
You must be tired.	intu laazim ta⁹baaniin.
It's very hot today.	il-yoom haara hwaaya.
Would you like some cold water?	triiduun mayy baarid?
Kaamil, give them some cold water.	Kaamil, intiihum mayy baarid.
With pleasure.	⁹ala ⁹eini.
Good-bye.	ma⁹a s-salaama.

Demonstration (muzaahara)

administrator	idaari
angry	ghazbaan
barbed wire	aslaak shaakka
crowd	tajammu⁹
dangerous	khatar
demonstration	muzaahara
hostile demonstration	*muzaahara ⁹idaa'iyya*
military demonstration	*muzaahara ⁹askariyya*
peaceful demonstration	*muzaahara silmiyya*
employee/s	muwazzaf/muwazzafiin
injured	majruuh

killed (*adj.*)	maqtuul
looking for (we are)	nfattish ⁹an
peace	silim, slaam
rioting	shaghab
rocks	hjaar
sabotage	takhriib
saboteurs	mukharribiin
search, inspection	taftiish
security	amin
security police	shurtat amin
shots	talqaat
warning shots	*talqaat tah dhiir*
Stay away!	ubqa liighaad!
strike	izraab
threat	khatar
threatened	fii khatar
traffic	muruur
U.S. administration	il-'idaara l-amriikiyya
U.S. aid	il-Musaa⁹daat il-amriikiyya
worker/s	⁹aamil/⁹ummaal

You, mister!	yaa sayyid!
What is that crowd?	shunu haadha it-tajammu⁹?
Is it a demonstration?	haadhi muzaahara?
What is it about?	hawl shunu?
What do you (*pl.*) want?	sh-itriiduun?
Are you military or civil employees?	intu ⁹askar loo muwazzafiin?
Disperse!	tfarqu!

Move!	ith̲ark! (*sing.*)/ith̲arku! (*pl.*)
Don't move!	la-tith̲arrak! (*sing.*)/ la-tith̲arrku! (*pl.*)
Don't shoot!	la-tutluq in-naar!
You, stop!	inta, oogfu!
You, move forward!	inta, ta⁹aal!
You, stay away!	inta, ubqa liig̲haad!
Go away!	ruuh lig̲haad!
You, go away!	inta, ruuh liig̲haad!
Don't pass the barbed wire!	la-t⁹ubruun l-aslaak ish-shaakka!
It's dangerous!	haadha khatar!
I want you to disperse!	ariidkum titfarquun!
Go home now!	ruuhu li-byuutkum hissa!
Tomorrow, we will solve the problem.	baachir, n̲hill il-mushkila.
No screaming!	maaku s̲yaah̲!
Stop throwing rocks!	wagfu ramy li-h̲jaar!
These are warning shots!	haadh̲i talqaat tah̲ dh̲iir!
We don't want anybody to get hurt.	ma-nriid ayy waahid yitadh̲dh̲a.
Go! Go! Go!	ruuh̲u! ruuh̲u! ruuh̲u! (*pl.*)
Traffic must pass.	il-muruur laazim yimshi.
Thank you, thank you.	shukran, shukran.

Searching a House (taftiish beit)

Baathist/s	Ba⁹thi/Ba⁹thiyyiin
cooperation	ta⁹aawin

help (*n.*)	musaa9ada
help (*v.*)	ysaa9id
house	beit
party (political)	hizib
party member	hizbi
political party	hizib siyaasi
roof	satih
soldier/s	jundi/junuud
weapon/s	slaah/asliha

Who is at the door?	minu bil-baab?
We are American military.	ihna 9askar Amriiki.
Open the door quickly!	iftahu l-baab bi-sur9a!
What's the matter?	shaku?
Hello.	marhaba.
Please, don't move around!	rajaa'an, la-titharrkuun!
Stay over there!	ibqu hnaak!
Don't lie to us!	la-tkidhbuun 9aleina!
We are here to help you.	ihna hnaa hatta nsaa9idkum.

We are here looking for Baathists.	ihna hnaa nfattish 9an Ba9thiyyiin.
looters.	*nahhaaba.*
party members.	*hizbiyyiin.*
saboteurs.	*mukharribiin.*
thieves.	*haraamiyya.*
weapons.	*asliha.*
Do you have weapons in the house?	9idkum asliha bil-beit?

Are you Baathists?	intu Ba⁹thiyyiin?
Do you know any Baathists?	tu⁹urfuun ayy Ba⁹thiyyiin?
saboteurs?	*mukharribiin?*
What is in that room?	shaku b-haadhi l-ghurfa?
What is in that box?	shaku b-haadha s-sanduug?
What is behind that?	shaku wara haadha?
Do you have anything on the roof?	aku shi ⁹as-satih?
We must take you with us for questioning.	laazim naakh dhak wiyyaana lit-tahqiiq.
Don't be afraid.	la-tkhaaf.
We just want to ask you a few questions.	nriid nisi'lak cham su'aal.
Do you need anything?	mihtaajiin shii?
Thank you for your cooperation.	shukran il-ta⁹aawinkum wiyyaana.
Good-bye.	ma⁹a s-salaama.

Public Services

Basic Words and Phrases

architect	mi⁹maari
assistance, help	musaa⁹ada
assistant	musaa⁹id
Baghdadis	ahal ba<u>gh</u>daad, b<u>gh</u>aada
builder	banna
building	binaaya
high-rise	*⁹imaara*
chemicals	kiimyaawiyyaat, mawaad
	kiimyaawiyya
chemist	kiimyaawi
company	sharika
dirt	wa<u>s</u>aa<u>kh</u>a
drink (*v.*)	yishrab
electric/electrician	kahrabaa'i
electricity	kahrabaa'
electrified	mkahrab
electric generator	muwallida kahrabaa'iyya
electric transformer	mu<u>h</u>awwila kahrabaa'iyya
electric wires	aslaak kahrabaa'iyya
engineer	muhandis
enough	kaafi, kifaaya
full	malyaan
garbage, trash	zibil, zbaala
garbage dump	mazbala
garbage truck	loory zbaala
health	<u>s</u>i<u>hh</u>a

139

healthy	sihhi
hospital	mustashfa
lab	mukhtabar
machines, equipment	makaayin
manager	mudiir, ra'iis
maybe, perhaps	yimkin
Ministry of Health	Wazaarat is-Sihha
municipality	baladiyya
Municipality Department	Mudiriyyat il-Baladiyyaat
must, have to	laazim
Office of Reconstruction and Humanitarian Assistance (in Iraq)	Maktab I⁹aadat il-I⁹maar wil-Musaa⁹adaat il-Insaaniyya
pipe	inbuub, buuri
public services	khadamaat ⁹aama
reconstruction	i⁹aadat i⁹maar
repair	tasliih
representative	mumaththil, manduub
scientist	⁹aalim
temperature	darajat il-haraara
unhealthy	muu sihhi
water/s	mayy/miyaah
clear water	*mayy saafi*
contaminated water	*mayy mulawwath*
drinking water	*mayy shurub*
muddy water	*mayy khaabut*
water purification plant	ma⁹mal tasfiyat miyaah
water supply	tajhiizaat miyaah
water truck	loory miyaah

work	^{9}amal, shughul
worker	^{9}aamil

Water Purification Plant (ma^{9}mal tasfiyat miyaah)

Where is the water purification plant?	wein ma^{9}mal tasfiyat il-miyaah?
Is that the plant?	haadha huwwa l-ma^{9}mal?
Is it working or not?	huwwa yushtughul loo laa?
Why isn't it working?	leish ma-yushtughul?
The machines are broken.	il-makaayin mkassra.
The water in the tanks is contaminated.	mayy il-ahwaaz mulawwath.
Don't drink that water!	la-tshirbuun haadha il-mayy!
Take a sample to the lab.	ukhudh ^{9}ayyina lil-mukhtabar.
Where is Engineer Ali?	wein il-muhandis Ali?
Engineer Ali, please get the workers.	muhandis Ali, rajaa'an jiib il-^{9}ummaal.
You must repair the machines.	laazim tsalhuun il-makaa'in.
in one week.	*bi-sbuu^9 waahid.*
in two weeks.	*bi-sbuu^{9}ein.*
People must have healthy, clear water.	in-naas laazim tishrab mayy sihhi w-saafi.
We need more chlorine.	nihtaaj klooriin akthar.
I'll call the Office of Reconstruction.	rah-akhaabur Maktab I^{9}aadat il-I^{9}maar.
Do you need anything else?	tihtaajuun shii aakhar?

141

We need chemicals.	nihtaaj kiimyaawiyyaat.
pipes.	*bwaari.*
water trucks.	*looriyyaat miyaah.*
We must work hard.	laazim nushtughul b-jidd.
Let's begin work.	yalla lil-⁹amal.
You clean the tanks.	intu nazzufu l-ahwaaz.
And you repair the machines.	wintu sallihu l-makaayin.
People are waiting for clear water.	in-naas bi-ntizaar il-mayy is-saafi.
God may help them.	alla yasaa⁹idhum.

Electric Generator (*muwallida kahrabaa'iyya*)

There is no electricity in Mansour.	maaku kahrabbaa' bil-Mansuur.
Electricity breaks down every hour.	il-kahrabaa' tingiti⁹ kull saa⁹a.
Where is the Mansour electric generator?	wein miwallidat kahrabaa' il-Mansuur?
We must increase its power capacity.	laazim nziid taaqat-ha l-kahrabaai'yya.
Inspect the electrical unit.	ifhas il-wihda l-kahrabaa'iyya.
to find what the problems are.	*hatta nu⁹ruf il-mashaakil.*
Write me a report with your needs.	iktibli taqriir bi-htiyaajaatak.
You may need cables.	yimkin tihtaaj kablaat.
one more electrician.	*kahrabaa'i aakhar.*
transformers.	*muhawwilaat.*
wires.	*aslaak.*

Where is Engineer Waleed?	wein il-muhandis Waliid?
We may have to enlarge the electrical network.	yimkin laazim nwassi⁹ ish-shabaka il-kahrabaa'iyya.
Tomorrow we are receiving electric supplies.	baachir, nistilim mu⁹iddaat kahrabaa'iyya.
Summer is very hot in Baghdad.	is-seif kullish haar ib-Baghdaad.
Especially in the month of July.	khusuusan ib-shahar Tammuuz.
Baghdadis must get enough electricity to keep air conditioners working.	ahal Baghdaad laazim yhasluun kahrabaa' kaafya hatta tshaghghil il-mubarridaat.
This summer is hell!	haadha Seif jahannam!
May God help people.	alla ysaa⁹id in-naas.

Trash Service Office (maktab khadamaat li-zbaala)

Hello.	marhaba.
I'd like to see the office manager, Mr. Sami.	ariid ashuuf mudiir il-maktab, sayyid Saami.
I am Sami. What is the matter?	aani Saami. shunu il-mawzuu⁹?
I am from the U.S. Office of Reconstruction.	aani min Maktab I⁹aadat il-I⁹maar il-Amriiki.
And with me is Mr. Clark from the United Nations.	wa wiyyaaya sayyid Klaark min Munazzamat il-Umam il-Muttahida.
Welcome. Please sit down.	ahlan wa sahlan. tfazzalu stiriihu.
Thank you.	shukran.

God bless.	allaa bil-kheir.
God bless. (in reply)	alla bil-kheir.
No, please, no tea.	laa, rajaa'an, ma-laazim chaay.
I'd like to inform you that the city is full of trash.	nhibb nkhubrak il-madiina malyaana zbaala.
The condition is very unhealthy.	il-haala kullish muu sihhiyya.
Our offices are unhappy about that.	makaatibna muu raazya ⁹an haadhi l-wasaakha.
We brought two garbage trucks with us.	jibna wiyyaana looriyyein liz-zibaala.
You must begin cleaning immediately.	laazim tibdi it-tanziif haalan.
We hope that you will begin work in Republic Square.	narju tibdi il-⁹amal min Saahat il-Jamhuuriyya.
This is a map to the garbage dump.	haadhi khariita li-makaan rami li-zbaala.
Do you need anything?	tihtaaj ay shii?
Please let us know when you need anything.	rajaa'an, ukhburna min tihtaaj ay shii.
We want to see the city clean.	nriid nshuuf il-madiina naziifa.
in order to breathe fresh air.	*hatta nishtamm hawa naqi.*
Thank you for your cooperation.	shukran ⁹ala ta⁹aawnak wiyyaana.
Good-bye.	ma⁹a s-salaama.

Chapter **5**

English–Iraqi Arabic Dictionary

In this dictionary nouns and adjectives are listed in their singular (*sing.*) and plural (*pl.*) forms, as well as the masculine (*m.*) and feminine (*f.*) forms when appropriate. The definite article **il-** (**the**) has been omitted. Verbs are given in the third-person masculine form (he) in the past tense followed by the present tense. The root verb type—regular (*rv*), double (*dv*), hollow (*hv*), or weak (*wv*)—or the imperative (*iv*) is then indicated to help the reader find the verb's conjugation in Chapter 1. Note that "/s" is used with English nouns merely as a symbol to indicate the plural form, even though that plural form may be spelled differently, as in "woman" and "women."

A

Abbasid Palace	il-Qasr il-ˁabbaasi
about	ˁann, hawl
accident/s	haaditha/hawaadith
car accident	*haadithat sayyaara*

account/s	ḥsaab/ḥisaabaat
adapter/s	muḥawwila/muḥawwilaat
address/s	9unwaan/9anaawiin
adjacent	yamm
administrator/s	idaari/idaariyyiin
afraid, to be afraid	khaaf/ykhaaf (*hv*)
Africa	Afriiqya
after	ba9ad
afternoon, early	9aṣir
afternoon, late	masaa'
Agargouf (ancient city near Baghdad)	Agarguuf
age/s	9umur/a9maar
agency/s	wakaala/wakaalaat, hay'a/hay'aat
air	hawa, hawaa'
fresh air	*hawa naqi*
air conditioner/s	mubarrida/mubarridaat
airlines	khuṭuuṭ ṭayyaraan
Iraqi Airlines	*Khuṭuuṭ iṭ-Ṭayyaraan il-9iraaqiyya*
airplane/s	ṭayyaara/ṭayyaaraat
airport/s	maṭaar/maṭaaraat
Baghdad International Airport	*Maṭaar Baghdaad id-Duwali*
all	kull
also	ayẓan, hamein
although	walaw
A.M.	ṣabaaḥan
ambulance	sayyaarat is9aaf

America	Amriika
North America	*Amriika ish-Shimaaliyya*
South America	*Amriika ij-Junuubiyya*
American	Amriiki (*m.*)/Amriikaan
	Amriikiyya (*f.*)/Amriikiyyaat
amount/s	mablagh/mabaaligh
ancient	qadiim (*m.*)
	qadiima (*f.*)
ancient mound	tall athari
and	wa/w-
angry	ghazbaan (*m.*)/ghazbaaniin
	ghazbaana (*f.*)/ghazbaanaat
another	aakhar, laakh
antiquities	aathaar
appetizers	mazza
appointment/s	maw⁹id/mawaa⁹iid
Arab (*n.*)	⁹arabi (*m.*)/⁹arab
	⁹arabiyya (*f.*)/⁹arabiyyaat
Arabic language	il-lugha il-⁹arabiyya
Arak (national Iraqi drink)	⁹arag
archaeological expedition	bi⁹tha athariyya
archaeological site	mawqi⁹ athari
archaeologist	aathaari (*m.*)/aathaariyyiin
	aathaariyya (*f.*)/aathaariyyiin
archaeology	aathaar
architect/s	mi⁹maari/mi⁹maariiyyiin
are, is	hal
arm/s	dhiraa⁹/adhru⁹
army/s	jaysh/juyuush

arrange	nazzam/ynazzum (*rv*)
arrival	wusuul
art/s	fann/funuun
Asia	Aasya
ask	si'al/yis'al (*rv*)
assistance	musaa⁹ada
assistant/s	musaa⁹id (*m.*)/musaa⁹idiin
	musaa⁹ida (*f.*)/musaa⁹idaat
at, by, in	b-/bi-
at [someone's] place	⁹ind
aunt/s (maternal)	khaala/khaalaat
aunt/s (paternal)	⁹mma/⁹mmaat
automated teller machine	aalat sahb fluus
automatic	otoomaatiiki
autumn	il-Khariif
available	mitwaffir

B

Baathist/s	Ba⁹thi (*m.*)/Ba⁹thiyyiin
	Ba⁹thiyya (*f.*)/Ba⁹thiyyaat
Babylon	Baabil
Babylonians (people of ancient Mesopotamia)	Baabiliyyiin
back (*n.*)	zahar
bag/s	junta/junat
paper bag	*chiis*
Baghdad	Baghdaad
Baghdad International Airport	Mataar Baghdaad id-Duwali

Baghdadi/s	Baghdaadi (*m.*)/Bghaada
	Baghdaadiyya (*f.*)/Bghaada
baked	makhbuuz
bakery/s	makhbaz/makhaabuz
bank/s	bank/bnuuk, masraf/masaarif
Central Bank	*il-Bank il-Markazi*
Rafidain Bank	*Bank ir-Raafidein*
bar/s	baar/baaraat
barbed wire	aslaak shaakka
barber/s	hallaaq/hallaaqiin, mzayyin/
	mzayyniin
bargaining	mu⁹aamala
basic	asaasi
basketball	kurat is-salla
bathroom	hammaam
battery/s	baatri/baatriyyat
beard/s	lihya/lihaa
beautiful	jamiil (*m.*)
	jamiila (*f.*)
because	li-an
bed/s	siriir/asirra
beer	biira
before	gabul
begin	bida/yibdi (*wv*)
behind	wara
beside	yamm
better	ahsan
between	bein
big, large	chibiir (*m.*)/kbaar
	chibiira (*f.*)/kbaar

bill	ḥsaab
birthday	mawlid, ⁹iid miilaad
black	aswad (*m.*)
	sooda (*f.*)
black market	suug sooda
blanket/s	baṭṭaaniyya/baṭṭaaniyyat
blond	ashgar (*m.*)
	shagra (*f.*)
blood	damm
blue	azrag (*m.*)
	zarga (*f.*)
boat/s	balam/blaam, qaarib/qawaarib
sailboat	*balam shiraa⁹i*
boat trip	riḥla b-qaarib
body/s	jisim/ajsaam
boiled	masluug (*m.*)
	masluuga (*f.*)
bone/s	⁹aẓum/⁹ẓaam
book/s	ktaab/kutub
bookstore	maktaba, makhzan kutub
border	ḥuduud
border crossing	ma⁹bar ḥuduud
bowl/s	ṭaasa/ṭaasaat, kaasa/kaasaat
box/s	ṣanduug/ṣanaadiig
boxing	mulaakama
brakes	breikaat
bread (flat)	khubuz
bread (Italian loaf)	sammuun
pieces of bread	*guraṣ khubuz*

150

break	kisar/yiksir (*rv*), gita^9/yigta^9 (*rv*)
breakfast	rayyuug, futuur
brick/s	taabuuga/taabuug
bridge/s	jisir/jsuur
bring	jaab/yjiib (*hv*)
broadcaster/s	mudhii^9 (*m.*)/mudhii^{9}iin
	mudhii^{9}a (*f.*)/mudhii^{9}aat
broiled, grilled	mashwi
broken	maksuur (*m.*)/mkasra,
	kharbaan (*m.*)/kharbaaniin
	maksuura (*f.*)/mkasra,
	kharbaana (*f.*)/kharbaanaat
brother/s	akh/ukhwaan
brown	joozi (*m.*)/jooziyya
	asmar (*m.*)/sumur
	samra (*f.*)/samraat
brush/s	fircha/firach
builder/s	banna/bannaa'iin
building/s	binaaya/binaayaat
high-rise/s	^{9}imaara/^{9}imaaraat
bulb/s	lampa/lampaat
bus/s	paas/paasaat
bus stop	mawqif paas
business/s	^{9}amal/a^{9}maal
business-class ticket	butaaqa daraja uulaa
businessman	rajul a^{9}maal
busy	mashghuul (*m.*)/mashghuuliin
	mashghuula (*f.*)/mashghuulaat
but	laakin, bass

buy	ishtira/yishtiri (*wv*)
by, at, in	b-/bi-

C

cabin/s	kaabiina/kaabiinaat
cables	kablaat
cafeteria	kaaftirya
Caliphs' Mosque	Jaami⁹ il-Khulafaa'
call	khaabar/ykhaabur (*rv*)
call/s (phone)	mukaalama/mukaalamaat
international call	*mukaalama duwaliyya*
local call	*mukaalama mahalliyya*
camera/s	kamira/kaamiraat
camp/s	mukhayyam/mukhayyamaat
can/s	quutiyya/qwaati
cancel	ligha/yilghi (*wv*)
canceling	ilghaa'
car/s	sayyaara/sayyaaraat
car license	*raqam sayyaara*
driver's license	*ijaazat siyaaqa*
car rental	*ta'jiir sayyaaraat*
carat	qiiraat
careful	diir baalak (*m.*)/diiru baalkum
	diiri baalich (*f.*)/diiru baalkum
cart/s	⁹arabaana/⁹arabaanaat
cashier	sarraaf (*m.*)/sarraafiin
	sarraafa (*f.*)/sarraafaat
casino	gaaziino

centimeter/s	santimatir/santimatraat
cereal	hubuub
change/s	taghyiir/taghyiiraat
change	ghayyar/yghayyir (*hv*)
cheap	rikhiis (*m.*)/rkhaas
	rikhiisa (*f.*)/rkhaas
check/s	chakk/chukuuk, sakk/sukuuk
personal check	*chakk shakh si*
check-in	nuzuul
check-out	mughaadara
check up	fuhas/yifhas (*rv*)
checking account	hsaab jaari
checkpoint/s	nuqtat taftiish/nuqaat taftiish
chemicals	kiimyaawiyyaat/mawaad
	kiimaawiyya
chemist	kiimyaawi
chest	sadir
chicken/s	dijaaja/dijaaj
children	atfaal, awlaad
chlorine	klooriin
Christmas	Krismis
church/s	kaniisa/kanaa'is
cinema/s	siinama/siinamaat
city/s	madiina/mudun
civil	madani (*m.*)/madaniyyiin
	madaniyya (*f.*)/madaniyyiin
clay, adobe	tiin
clean	naziif (*m.*)
	naziifa (*f.*)

clean	nazzaf/ynazzuf (*rv*)
clinic/s	mustawsif/mustawsafaat,
	⁹iyaada/⁹iyaadaat
clock/s	saa⁹a/saa⁹aat
close	sadd/ysidd (*dv*)
close by	qariib, yamm
clothes	malaabis
clothing store	mahal malaabis
cloud/s	gheima/ghuyuum
club/s	naadi/nawaadi
nightclub	*naadi leili, malha*
social club	*naadi ijtimaa⁹i*
sports club	*naadi riyaazi*
coffee	gahwa
coffee shop/s	gahwa/gahaawi
cold	baarid (*m.*)
	baarda (*f.*)
color/s	loon/alwaan
come	ija/yiji (*hv*)
coming	jaay (*m.*)/jaayyiin
	jaayya (*f.*)/jaayyaat
company/s	sharika/shariikaat
concerned	yhimm
concert/s (music)	hafla moosiiqiyya/haflaat
	moosiiqiyya
congratulations	mabruuk
continent/s	qaara/qaaraat
contribute	tbarra⁹/yitbarra⁹ (*rv*)

cook/s	tabbaakh (*m.*)/tabbaakhiin
	tabbaakha (*f.*)/tabbaakhaat
cook	tubakh/yutbukh (*rv*)
cookbook	ktaab tabukh
cooperation	ta⁹aawin
copier	alat istinsaakh
copper	nuhaas, sifir
copying	istinsaakh
corner/s	zaawiya/zawaayaa
cost	si⁹ir, kilfa
cough	gahh/yguhh (*dv*)
country/s	balad/blaad, qutur/aqtaar
cover	ghatta/yghatti (*wv*)
credit card	bitaaqat i'timaan
crowd	tajummu⁹, jamaahiir
cuneiform writing	kitaaba mismaariyya
currency	⁹umla
hard currency	*⁹umla sa⁹ba*
currency exchange office	maktab tasriif
customs	gumrug
customs control	qisim il-gumrug

D

dance	rigis
dancer/s	raaqisa/raaqisaat
dangerous	khatar
dark (color)	tuukh
dark (night)	zalma

daughter/s	ibna/banaat, bint/banaat
day/s	yoom/ayyaam
day before yesterday	awwal il-baarha
delicious	ṭayyib
demonstration/s	muzaahara/muzaaharaat
hostile demonstration	*muzaahara ⁹idaa'iyya*
military demonstration	*muzaahara ⁹askariyya*
peaceful demonstration	*muzaahara silmiyya*
dentist	tabiib asnaan
Department of Travel and Naturalization	Mudiiriyyat is-Safar wij-Jinsiyya
departure	mughaadara
dictionary/s	qaamuus/qawaamiis
difficult	sa⁹ub (*m.*)
	sa⁹ba (*f.*)
dig/s	hafur/hafriyyaat
digger	haffaar, munaqqib
digging equipment	adawaat hafur
dinar/s (Iraqi currency)	dinaar/danaaniir
dinner	⁹asha
director/s	mudiir/mudaraa'
Directorate General of Antiquities (Baghdad)	Mudiiriyyat il-Aathaar il-⁹aama
dirt	wisakh
dirty	wasikh (*m.*)/waskhiin
	waskha (*f.*)/waskhaat
dish/s (food)	akla/aklaat
Disperse!	tfarqu!
ditch/s	hufra/hufar

diving	ghatis
divorced	mtallig (*m.*)/mtalgiin
	mtalliga (*f.*)/mtalgaat
dizziness	dookha
doctor/s	tabiib/atibbaa', diktoor/dakaatira
dog/s	chalib/chlaab
dollar/s	duulaar/duulaaraat
Don't move!	la-titharrak!/la-titharku!
Don't shoot!	la-tutluq in-naar!
downtown	markaz il-madiina
drawing/s	mukhattat, mukhattataat
dress	libas/yilbas (*rv*)
drink	shirab/yishrab (*rv*)
drinks	mashruubaat
drive	saaq/ysuuq (*hv*)
driver	saayiq (*m.*)/suwwaaq
	saayqa (*f.*)/saayqaat
driver's license	ijaazat siyaaqa
international license	*ijaaza ⁹aalamiyya*
driving	siyaaqa
dry	jaaf
dry cleaning	tanziif jaaf, kawi
dubbed film	filim mudablaj
dust	⁹ajaaj
dust storm	⁹aasifa turaabiyya
duty, responsibility	waajib
duty-free shop	makhzan suug hurra

E

ear/s	idhin/aadhaan
eardrops	gatrat idhin
East	sharq
Eastern	sharqi (*m.*)/sharqiyyiin
	sharqiyya (*f.*)/sharqiyyaat
easy	sahil (*m.*)/sahliin
	sahla (*f.*)/sahlaat
eat	akal/yaakul (*rv*)
economy	iqtisaad
economy-class ticket	bitaaqa daraja siyaahiyya
egg/s	beiza/beiz
electric/electrician	kahrabaa'i
electric generator	muwallida kahrabaa'iyya
electric transformer	muhawwila kahrabaa'iyya
electric wires	aslaak kahrabaa'iyya
electrical appliances	mu⁹iddaat kahrabaa'iyya
electricity	kahrabaa'
electrified	mkahrab
elevator/s	mas⁹ad/masaa⁹id
embassy/s	safaara/safaaraat
employee/s	muwazzaf (*m.*)/muwazzafiin
	muwazzafa (*f.*)/muwazzafaat
engaged	makh tuub (*m.*)
	makh tuuba (*f.*)
engineer/s	muhandis/muhandisiin
English language	il-lugha il-Ingiliiziyya
enough	kaafi, kifaaya

entrance/s	madkhal/madaakhi
entry	dukhuul
envelope/s	zaruf/zuruuf
equal	ysaawi
Euphrates River	Nahar il-Furaat
Euro	yooro
Europe	Awruppa
evening	leila
evening event	sahra
examination (medical)	fahis
examination (school)	ikhtibaar
excavation	tanqiibaat
excavator/s	munaqqib/munaqqibiin
excellent	mumtaaz (*m.*)/mumtaaziin
	mumtaaza (*f.*)/mumtaazaat
exchange	tasriif
exchange rate	si⁹ir it-tasriif
Excuse me./Excuse us.	⁹an idhnak. (*m.*)/⁹an idhinkum.
	⁹an idhnich. (*f.*)/⁹an idhinkum.
exhibit/s	ma⁹raz/ma⁹aariz
art exhibit	*ma⁹raz fanni*
exit	khuruuj
expedition/mission	bi⁹tha
expensive	ghaali (*m.*)/ghaaliin
	ghaalya (*f.*)/ghaalyaat
expire	intihat/tintihi (*wv*)
eye/s	⁹ein/⁹uyuun
eyedrops	gatra

F

fabric	qmaash
face/s	wijih/wijuuh
fall (season)	il-khariif
family/s	ahal, ⁹eila/⁹eilaat
far	bi⁹iid
fare	ujra
fast	sarii⁹ (*m.*)
	sarii⁹a (*f.*)
father	waalid, ab
fax	faaks
feel	shi⁹ar/yush⁹ur (*rv*)
fees	rusuum
feminine	mu'annath
festival/s	⁹iid/a⁹yaad
fiancée	khatiiba
field director	mudiir tanqiibaat
fill up	⁹abba/y⁹abbi (*wv*)
film/s	filim/aflaam
financial	maali
finger/s	isbi⁹/asaabi⁹
finish	khallas/ykhallis (*rv*)
first-class ticket	bitaaqa daraja uulaa
fish/s	simcha/simach
Masguf fish	*simach Masguuf*
fish, hunt	saad/ysiid (*hv*)
flashlight	flaash
flat tire	panchar
flight/s	rihla/rihlaat

flight check-in desk	maktab tasjiil ir-rihla
folk dance	rigis sha⁹bi
food	akil, ta⁹aam
Middle Eastern food	*akil sharqi*
traditional food	*akil sha⁹bi*
Western food	*akil gharbi*
foot/s	qadam/aqdaam
for, to	l-/li-, ili
foreman	us ta
forget	nisa/yinsa (*wv*)
form/s	istimaara/istimaaraat
fresh	taaza
friend/s	sadiiq/asdiqaa'
from	min
from . . . to	min . . . ilaa
front, in	amaam, giddam
fruits	fawaakih
full	malyaan (*m.*)/malyaaniin
	malyaana (*f.*)/malyaanaat
future	mustaqbal

G

garbage, trash	zibil, zbaala
garbage dump	mazbala
garbage truck	loori zbaala
gas	baanziin
premium gas	*baanziin mumtaaz*

gas station	mahattat baanziin, baanziinkhaana
gate	bawwaaba
gate number	raqam il-bawwaaba
general	^{9}aam (*m.*)
	^{9}aama (*f.*)
general information	ma^{9}luumaat ^{9}aama
get	jaab/yjiib (*hv*)
gift/s	hadiyya/hadaayaa
Gilgamesh (ancient king and hero)	Gilgaamish
glass	jaam, zujaaj
glasses (eye)	nazaaraat, manaazir
Go!	ruuh! (*m.*)/ruuhu! (*iv*)
	ruuhi! (*f.*)/ruuhu!
Go away.	ruuh liighaad. (*m.*)/ruuhu liighaad.
	ruuhi liighaad. (*f.*)/ruuhu liighaad.
God	alla
God bless	allaa bil-kheir
God may help you.	alla yasaa^{9}idkum.
God willing	inshaalla
going (participle)	raayih (*m.*)/raayhiin
	raayha (*f.*)/raayhaat
gold	zahab
good/s	zein (*m.*)/zeiniin
	zeina (*f.*)/zeinaat
Good afternoon.	masaa' il-kheir.

Good morning.	sabaah il-kheir.
Good night.	tisbah 9ala kheir. (*m.*)/
	tisbahuun 9ala kheir.
	tisbahiin 9ala kheir. (*f.*)/
	tisbahuun 9ala kheir.
Good-bye.	ma9a s-salaama.
gram	ghraam
grandfather	jidd
grandmother	jidda
grave/s	gabur/gubuur
gray	rumaadi (*m.*)
	rumaadiyya (*f.*)
great	9aziim (*m.*)
	9aziima (*f.*)
green	akh zar (*m.*)
	khazra (*f.*)
greeting/s	tahiyya/tahiyyaat
group/s	firqa/firaq
guide	daliil
guidebook	daliil siyaahi
gulf	khaliij
gynecologist	tabiib nisaa'iyyaat

H

hair	sha9ar
haircut	zyaan
hairdresser	hallaaq, mzayyin
half	nuss

hand/s	iid/aydi
hanger/s	ti⁹laaga/ti⁹laagaat
hard currency	⁹umla sa⁹ba
have	⁹ind
he	huwwa
head/s	raas/ruus
health	sihha
healthy	sihhi
hear	sima⁹/yisma⁹ (*rv*)
heart/s	galub/gluub
heavy	thigiil (*m.*)/thgaal
	thigiila (*f.*)/thgaal
hello, hi	marhaba
help (*n.*)	musaa⁹ada
help	saa⁹ad/ysaa⁹id (*rv*)
here	hnaa
highway	tariiq sarii⁹
history	taariikh
hoe	mishaa
holiday/s	⁹utla/⁹utal
honor	sharaf
honored	tsharrafna
(The) honor is ours. (reply)	wilna sh-sharaf.
hospital/s	mustashfa/mustashfayaat
hot	haar (*m.*)
	haarra (*f.*)
hotel/s, motel/s	findiq/fanaadiq
hour/s	saa⁹a/saa⁹aat
house/s	beit/byuut

How?	shloon?
How far?	shgadd?
How long?	shgadd?
How many?	kam?, cham?
How much?	shgadd?, ibbeish?
humid	ratub (*m.*)
	ratba (*f.*)
hungry	juu⁹aan (*m.*)/juu⁹aaniin
	juu⁹aana (*f.*)/juu⁹aanaat
Hurry!	b-sur⁹a!
Hurry up!	yalla!
hurt (to get)	tadhdha/yitadhdha (*wv*)
husband/s	zooj/azwaaj

I

I (am)	aani
if	loo, idha
illegal	mamnuu⁹ (*m.*)/mamnuu⁹iin
	mamnuu⁹a (*f.*)/mamnuu⁹aat
illegal items	ashyaa' mamnuu⁹a
imitation	taqliid
immediately	haalan
important	muhim
in a hurry	mista⁹jil (*m.*)/mista⁹jiliin
	mista⁹jila (*f.*)/mista⁹jilaat
in front of	giddaam
inch/s	inch/inchaat

indebted	mamnuun (*m.*)/mamnuuniin
	mamnuuna (*f.*)/mamnuunaat
inexpensive	muu ghaali
infection/s	iltihaab/iltihaabaat
information	isti⁹laamaat, ma⁹luumaat
information office	maktab isti⁹laamaat
injured (person)	majruuh (*m.*)/majruuhiin
	majruuha (*f.*)/majruuhaat
inside	daakhil, jawwa
inspection	taftiish
insurance	ta'miin
car insurance	*ta'miin sayyaraat*
health insurance	*ta'miin sihhi*
international	⁹aalami (*m.*)/⁹aalamiyyiin
	⁹aalamiyya (*f.*)/⁹aalamiyyaat
Internet	intarnat
introduction	ta⁹aaruf
investigation	tahqiiq
invite	da⁹a/yid⁹u (*wv*)
Iraq	⁹iraaq
Iraqi	⁹iraaqi (*m.*)/⁹iraaqiyyiin
	⁹iraaqiyya (*f.*)/⁹iraaqiyyaat
is/are	hal-
island/s	jaziira/juzur

J

jeweler/s	saayigh/siyyaagh
jogging	harwala

journalism	sahaafa, i⁹laam
journalist/s	sahafi (*m.*)/sahafiyyiin
	sahafiyya (*f.*)/sahafiyyaat
journalistic report/news story	taqriir sahafi
juice	⁹asiir
apple juice	*⁹asiir tuffaah*
carrot juice	*⁹asiir jizar*
orange juice	*⁹asiir burtuqaal*

K

key/s	miftaah/mafaatiih
killed (*adj.*)	maqtuul (*m.*)/maqtuuliin
	maqtuula (*f.*)/maqtuulaat
kilo/s	keilo/keilowwaat
half a kilo	*nuss keilo*
quarter of a kilo	*rubu⁹ keilo*
kilogram/s	keilo ghraam/keilo ghraamaat
kitchen/s	matbakh/mataabukh
knife/s	sichchiin/sichaachiin
know	⁹iraf/yu⁹ruf (*rv*)

L

lab/s	mukhtabar/mukhtabaraat
lab test/s	tahliil/tahaaliil
Labor Day	⁹iid il-⁹ummaal
lake/s	buhayra/buhayraat

landmarks	ma⁹aalim
large	chibiir (*m.*)/kbaar
	chibiira (*f.*)/kbaar
late	mit'akhkhir (*m.*)/mit'akhriin
	mit'akhra (*f.*)/mit'akhraat
later	ba⁹dein
laundry	ghasil, makwa
pressing, ironing	*kawi*
lavatory, toilet	mirhaaz, twaaleit
leave	tirak/yutruk (*rv*)
left	yisra
leg/s	rijil/arjul
lesson/s	daris/duruus
letter/s	risaala/rasaa'il
library/s	maktaba/makaatib
license/s	ijaaza/ijaazaat
driver's license	*ijaazat siyaaqa*
lie	kidhab/yikdhib (*rv*)
light/s	ziwa/azwiya
light (weight)	khafiif
like	habb/yhibb (*dv*)
line/s	khatt/khtuut
liter/s	latir/latraat
little	shwayya, qaliil
local	mahalli (*m.*)/mahalliyyiin
	mahalliyya (*f.*)/mahalliyyaat
location/s	mawqi⁹/mawaaqi⁹
long	tawiil (*m.*)/twaal
	tawiila (*f.*)/twaal

look for	fattash/yfattish (*rv*)
looter/s	naahib/nahhaaba
lose	zayya⁹/yzayyi⁹ (*hv*)
lost	zaayi⁹ (*m.*), mafquud (*m.*)/
	mafquudiin
	zaay⁹a (*f.*), mafquuda (*f.*)/
	mafquudaat
love	habb/yhibb (*dv*)
luggage, suitcase/s	junta/junat

M

machine/s	makiina/makaayin
magazine/s	majalla/majallaat
mail	bariid
airmail	*bariid jawwi*
express mail	*bariid sarii⁹*
registered mail	*bariid musajjal*
regular mail	*bariid ⁹aadi*
mailbox	sanduug bariid
mailman	postachi, abu l-bariid
man/s	rijjaal/ryaajiil
manager/s	mudiir (*m.*)/mudaraa’,
	ra’iis/ru’asaa’
	mudiira (*f.*)/mudiiraat
map/s	khariita/kharaayit
market/s	suug/aswaag
food market	*suug khuzrawaat*

169

married	mizzawwij (*m.*)/mizzawjiin
	mizzawja (*f.*)/mizzawjaat
martyr/s	shahiid (*m.*)/shuhadaa'
	shahiida (*f.*)/shahiidaat
masculine	mudhakkar
math	hisaab, riyaaziyyaat
matter/s	mawzuu⁹/mawaazii⁹
maybe, perhaps	yimkin, mumkin
measurement/s	qiyaas/qiyaasaat
meat	laham
mechanic	miikaaniiki (*m.*)
	miikaaniikiyya (*f.*)
mechanic's shop	mahal miikaaniiki
media	i⁹laam
medical	tibbi (*m.*)
	tibbiyya (*f.*)
medical care	⁹inaaya tibbiyya
medicine/s	diwa/adwiya
meeting	ijtimaa⁹, muqaabala
member/s	⁹uzu/a⁹zaa'
menu	manyo
metal/s	ma⁹dan/ma⁹aadin
meter/s	matir/amtaar
middle	wasat
Middle East, the	ish-Sharq il-Awsat
mile/s	miil/amyaal
military (*adj.*)	⁹askari (*m.*)/⁹askariyyiin
	⁹askariyya (*f.*)/⁹askariyyaat
milk	haliib

minaret/s	manaara/manaayir
minister/s	waziir/wuzaraa'
ministry/s	wizaara/wizaaraat
Ministry of Defense	Wizaarat id-Difaa⁹
Ministry of Health	Wazaarat is-Sihha
minute/s	daqiiqa/daqaayiq
Miss	aanisa
missing	mafquud (*m.*)/mafquudiin
	mafquuda (*f.*)/mafquudaat
mistake/s	ghalta/aghlaat
moderate	mu⁹tadil
modern	hadiith (*m.*)
	hadiitha (*f.*)
money	fluus
money orders	hawaala bariidiyya
month/s	shahar/ashhur
moon	gumar
more	akthar
morning	sabaah, subuh
mosque/s	jaami⁹/jawaami⁹
motel/s, hotel/s	findiq/fanaadiq
mother/s	umm, waalda
mound/s	tall/tluul
mouth/s	halig/hluug
Move!	itharrak! (*m.*)/itharrku! (*iv*)
	itharrki! (*f.*)/itharrku!
Move forward!	tqaddam! (*m.*)/tqaddmu! (*iv*)
	tqaddmi! (*f.*)/tqaddmu!
movie/s	filim/aflaam

Mr.	sayyid
Mrs.	sayyida
much	hwaaya
mud brick/s	libna/libin
municipality/s	baladiyya/baladiyyaat
Municipality Department	Mudiriyyat il-Baladiyyaat
museum/s	mathaf/mataahif
Iraqi Museum	*il-Mathaf il-⁹iraaqi*
music	moosiiqa
Eastern music	*moosiiqa sharqiyya*
Western music	*moosiiqa gharbiyya*
music concert	hafla moosiiqiyya
must	laazim
mustache	shwaarub

N

nation	watan
national	watani (*m.*)/wataniyyiin
	wataniyya (*f.*)/wataniyyaat
National Insurance Company	Sharikat it-Ta'miin il-Wataniyya
National Tourist Bureau	Maktab is-Siyaaha il-Wataniyya
nationalist	watani
nationality	jinsiyya
near	qariib
Near East, the	ish-Sharq il-Awsat
Near Eastern	sharqi (*m.*)/sharqiyyiin
	sharqiyya (*f.*)/sharqiyyaat
neck	rugba

need	h̲taaj/yih̲taaj (*hv*)
new	jdiid (*m.*)/jdaad
	jdiida (*f.*)/jdaad
New Year, the	⁹iid Raas is-Sana
news	ak̲hbaar
international news	*ak̲hbaar ⁹aalamiyya*
local news	*ak̲hbaar mah̲alliyya*
news bulletin	nashrat ak̲hbaar
newspaper/s	jariida/jaraayid, sah̲iifa/suh̲uf
newsstand	mah̲al jaraayid
next	jaay
next to	yamm
nice	zein (*m.*)/zeiniin
	zeina (*f.*)/zeinaat
night/s	leil/layaali
no	laa
nonsmoking section	qisim ⁹adam it-tadk̲hiin
noon	iz-zuhur
nose	k̲hashim, anff
not	muu/maa
now	hissa
number/s	raqam/arqaam
nurse/s	mumarriza/mumarrizaat

O

object/s	maadda/mawaad
occupation	shug̲hul, waziifa
ocean	muh̲iit

office/s	maktab/makaatib
Office of Reconstruction and Humanitarian Assistance	Maktab I⁹aadat il-I⁹maar wil-Musaa⁹adaat il-Insaaniyya
officer/s	zaabut/zubbaat
official (*adj.*)	rasmi (*m.*)/rasmiyyiin
	rasmiyya (*f.*)/rasmiyyaat
official visit	ziyaara rasmiyya
oil	dihin
OK	maykhaalif
on, upon	⁹ala/⁹a-
on top of	foog, ⁹ala
one way	dhihaaban
open	fitah/yiftah (*rv*)
operator	baddaala, abu il-baddaala
optician	nazzaaraati, ⁹uweinati
or	loo, aw
order/s	amur/awaamir
original	asli (*m.*)/asliyyiin
	asliyya (*f.*)/asliyyaat
ought	laazim
over	foog
over there	hnaak

P

package/s	ruzma/ruzam
pain	wija⁹, alam
paint	subugh
palace/s	qasir/qusuur

Pardon me.	⁹afwan.
park (a car)	waggaf/ywagguf (*rv*)
parking lot	mawqif sayyaaraat
party/s (political)	hizib/ahzaab
party member/s	hizbi (*m.*)/hizbiyyiin
	hizbiyya (*f.*)/hizbiyyaat
pass	⁹ubar/yu⁹bur (*rv*)
passport/s	paasporti/paasportaat,
	jawaaz/jawaazaat
past	maazi, faat
patient/s	mariiz/marzaa
peace	silim, salaam
pen/s, pencil/s	qalam/qlaam
penny	filis
percent	nisba mi'awiyya
period	⁹asir, fatra
pharmacist	saydali
pharmacy/s	saydaliyya/saydaliyyaat
Ph.D./s	ustaadh, diktoor (*m.*)/dakaatira
phone/s	talafoon/talafoonaat
photo/s	suura/suwar
photo shop	mahal taswiir
photographer/s	musawwir/musawwiriin
phrase/s	is tilaah/is tiilaahaat
physician/s	tabiib/atibbaa'
pick/s	qazma/qazmaat
picture/s	suura/suwar
pill/s	habba/hubuub
pillow/s	makhadda/makhaadiid

pipe/s	inbuub/anaabiib, buuri/buuriyyat
place/s	mahal/mahallaat
plane/s	tayyaara/tayyaaraat
plate/s	maa⁹uun/mwaa⁹iin
plated	matli
play	li⁹ab/yil⁹ab (rv)
play/s	masrahiyya/masrahiyyaat
please	min fazlak, rajaa'an
P.M.	masaa'an
police	shurta, pooliis
police station	markaz shurta
political party	hizib siyaasi
pool/s	masbah/masaabih
popular	sha⁹bi (m.)/sha⁹biyyiin
	sha⁹biyya (f.)/sha⁹biyyaat
porter/s	hammaal/hmaamiil
post office	maktab bariid
postal orders	hawaala bariidiyya
postcard	postkard
pregnant	haamil
prescription/s	wasfa/wasfaat
present	haazir
price/s	si⁹ir/as⁹aar
prison/s	sijin/sijuun
private	khusuusi
problem/s	mushkila/mashaakil
program/s	barnaamij/baraamij
prophet/s	nabi/anbiyaa'

public	⁹aam
public services	khadamaat ⁹aamma
pump	mazakhkha, pamp
push	difa⁹/yidfa⁹ (*rv*)
put	hatt/yhutt (*dv*)

Q

quarter	rubu⁹
question/s	su'aal/as'ila
quick	sarii⁹ (*m.*)/sarii⁹iin
	sarii⁹a (*f.*)/sarii⁹aat
quickly	bi-sur⁹a

R

radio/s	raadyo/raadyowaat
radio station/s	idhaa⁹a/idhaa⁹aat
rain	mutar
read	qira/yiqra (*wv*)
receipt/s	wasil/wusuulaat
reconstruction	i⁹aadat i⁹maar
record store	mahal sharaayit
recorder/s	musajjil/musajjiilaat
red	ahmar (*m.*)/humur
	hamra (*f.*)/humur
relatives, family	ahal, aqriibaa'
religion/s	diin/adyaan

renew	jaddad/yjaddid (*dv*)
rent	ajjar/yajjir (*rv*)
repair/s	tasliih/tasliihaat
repair	sallah/ysallih (*rv*)
reporter/s	muraasil/muraasiliin
representative	mumaththil, manduub
reservation	hajiz
Resident's Department	Mudiiriyyat il-Iqaama
restaurant/s	mat⁹am/mataa⁹um
return	rija⁹/yirja⁹ (*rv*)
revolution/s	thawra/thawraat
right (direction)	yimna, yamiin
rioting	shaghab
river/s	nahar/anhaar
road/s	tariiq/turuq
roasted	mashwi, mhammar
rocks	hjaar
roof/s	satih/sutuuh
room/s	ghurfa/ghuraf
room service	khidmat il-ghuraf
round-trip	murajja⁹, dhihaaban wa iyaaban
ruins	aathaar, baqaaya

S

sabotage	takhriib
saboteurs	mukhrribiin
safe/s	qaasa/qaasaat
salad	zalaata

sample	⁹ayyina
sandal/s	na⁹aal/ni⁹il
savings	tawfiir
savings account	hsaab tawfiir
say	gaal/yguul (*hv*)
school/s	madrasa/madaaris
scientist/s	⁹aalim/⁹ulamaa'
scissors	mugass
screaming	syaah
sea	bahar
seal/s	khatam/akhtaam
cylinder seal	*khatam is tiwaani*
search	taftiish
season/s	mawsim/mawaasim
seat/s	maq⁹ad/maqaa⁹id
second	thaani (*m.*)
	thaanya (*f.*)
security	amin
security police	shurtat amin
see	shaaf/yshuuf (*hv*)
send	dazz/ydizz (*dv*)
sew	khayyat/ykhayyit (*hv*)
shall	rah-, ha-
she	hiyya
shoe/s	qundara/qanaadir
shoe shine	sabbaagh
shoemaker	qundarchi
shop/s	dukkaan/dakaakiin

short	qasiir (*m.*)/qsaar
	qasiira (*f.*)/qsaar
shot/s	talqa/talqaat
warning shots	*talqaat tah dhiir*
show/s	9ariz/9uruuz
show	shawwaf/yshawwif (*hv*)
shower (bath)	duush
sick	mariiz (*m.*)/marzaa
	mariiza (*f.*)/mariizaat
sickness	maraz
sign/s	9alaama/9alaamaat
silver	fuzza
since	min
singer/s	mughanni (*m.*)/mughanniin
	mughanniyya (*f.*)/
	mughanniyyaat
single	a9zab (*m.*)
	9izba (*f.*)
sister/s	ukhut/khawaat
sit down	istariih (*m.*)/istariihu (*iv*)
	istariihi (*f.*)/istariihu
site/s	mawqi9/mawaaqi9
size/s	qiyaas/qiyaasaat
sleep	naam/ynaam (*hv*)
slipper	na9al
slow	batii' (*m.*)/batii'iin
	batii'a (*f.*)/batii'aat
slow down	khaffaf/ykhaffuf (*dv*)

small	saghiir (*m.*)/sghaar, zghayir (*m.*) /zghaar
	saghiira (*f.*)/sghaar, zghayra (*f.*)/ zghaar
small change	khurda
smoking section	qisim it-tadkhiin
sneeze	⁹itas/yi⁹tus (*rv*)
snow	thalij
soap	saabuun
soccer	kurat il-qadam
soldier/s	jundi/jnuud
solve	hall/yhill (*dv*)
son/s	ibin/abnaa'
song/s	ughniya/aghaani
soon	qariiban
sorry	⁹afwan
souvenirs	tuhafiyyaat, tizkaaraat
speak	tkallam/yitkallam (*rv*), hicha/yihchi (*wv*)
spices	bhaaraat
spot/s	buq⁹a/buqa⁹
spring (season)	ir-Rabii⁹
square/s (shape)	murabba⁹/murabba⁹aat
square/s (park)	saaha/saahaat
stamp/s	taabi⁹/tawaabi⁹
station/s	mahatta/mahattaat
train station	*mahattat qitaar*
statue/s	timthaal/tamaathiil
stay	buqa/yubqa (*wv*)

Stay away!	ubqa lii<u>gh</u>aad! (*m.*)/ubqu lii<u>gh</u>aad! (*iv*)
	ubqi lii<u>gh</u>aad! (*f.*)/ubqu lii<u>gh</u>aad!
staying	baaqi (*m.*)/baaqiin
	baaqya (*f.*)/baaqyaat
staying at	naazil (*m.*)/naazliin
	naazla (*f.*)/naazlaat
steal	baag/ybuug (*hv*), siraq/yusruq (*rv*)
stolen	mabyuug, masruuq
stomach/s	mi⁹da/mi⁹daat
stone/s	<u>h</u>ajar/<u>h</u>jaar, <u>s</u>akhar
Stop!	oogaf! (*m.*)/oogfu! (*iv*)
	oogfi! (*f.*)/oogfu!
store/s	dukkaan/dakaakiin, ma<u>h</u>al/ ma<u>h</u>allaat, ma<u>kh</u>zan/ ma<u>kh</u>aazin
straight	⁹adil
street/s	shaari⁹/shawaari⁹
main street	*shaari⁹ ra'iisi*
secondary street	*shaari⁹ far⁹i*
strike/s	i<u>z</u>raab/i<u>z</u>raabaat
student/s	<u>t</u>aalib (*m.*)/<u>t</u>ullaab
	<u>t</u>aalba (*f.*)/<u>t</u>aalibaat
subtitled film	filim mutarjam
study	diras/yudrus (*rv*)
stuffed	ma<u>h</u>shi
suddenly	⁹ala <u>gh</u>afla

Sumer (ancient land in Mesopotamia)	Soomar
Sumerian	Soomari (*m.*)/Soomariyyiin
	Soomariyya (*f.*)/Soomariyyaat
summer	is-Seif
sun	shamis
sweetshop	dukkaan halawiyyaat
swim	sibah/yisbah (*rv*)
swimming	sibaaha
symptoms	a⁹raaz
syringe/s	huqna/huqan

T

table/s	meiz/myuuza
tablet/s	raqiim/ruqum
clay tablet	*raqiim tiini*
take	akhadh/yaakhudh (*rv*)
take (away)	wadda/ywaddi (*wv*)
taxi/s	taksi/taksiyyaat
taxi stop	mawqif taksi
tea/s	chaay/chaayaat
light tea	*chaay khafiif*
strong tea	*chaay thigiil*
sweet tea	*chaay hilu*
tea shop/s	gahwa/gahaawi
teacher/s	mu⁹allim (*m.*)/mu⁹allimiin
	mu⁹allima (*f.*)/mu⁹allimaat
teacup/s	istikaan/istikaanaat

telephone/s	talafoon/talafoonaat
tell	gaal/yguul (*hv*)
teller/s	sarraaf (*m.*)/sarraafiin
	sarraafa (*f.*)/sarraafaat
temperature	darajat il-haraara
temple/s	ma⁹bad/ma⁹aabid
tennis	tanis
tent/s	kheima/khiyam
textiles	nasiij
Thank you.	shukran.
thankful	mamnuun (*m.*)/mamnuuniin
	mamnuuna (*f.*)/mamnuunaat
thanks	shukran
theater/s	masrah/masaarih
theft/s	sariqa/sariqaat
there	hnaak
there is/are	aku
these	hadhoola
they	humma
thief/s	haraami/haraamiyya
third	thaalith (*m.*)
	thaaltha (*f.*)
thirsty	⁹atshaan (*m.*)/⁹atshaaniin
	⁹atshaana (*f.*)/⁹atshaanaat
this	haadha (*m.*), haadhi (*f.*)
threat, danger	khatar
threatened	fii khatar
throwing	rami
ticket/s	tikit/tiktaat, tadhkara/tadhaakir

ticket window	shubbaak tadhaakir
Tigris River	Nahar Dijla
time	waqit, wakit
tip	bakh shiish, ikraamiyya
tire/s	taayar/taayaraat
flat tire	*panchar*
tire, to get tired	ti⁹ab/yit⁹ab (*rv*)
tired	ta⁹baan (*m.*)/ta⁹baaniin
	ta⁹baana (*f.*)/ta⁹baanaat
to, for	l-/li-
today	il-yoom
together	suwa
toilet, lavatory	twaaleit, mirhaaz
Tomb of the Unknown Soldier	ij-Jundi l-majhuul
tomorrow	baachir
tongue/s	lisaan/alsina
tonight	il-leila
tooth/s	sin/asnaan
toothbrush	firchat asnaan
toothpaste	ma⁹joon asnaan
tour/s	rihla/rihlaat, jawla/jawlaat
tourism	siyaaha
tourist/s	saa'ih/suwwaah
towel/s	khawli/khaawliyyaat
town/s	madiina/mudun
traffic	muruur
traffic police	shurtat il-muruur
train/s	qitaar/qitaaraat
train station	mahattat qitaar

transformer/s	muwallida/muwallidaat
transit	muruur
translate	tarjam/ytarjum (*rv*)
translation/s	tarjama/taraajum
translator/s	mutarjim (*m.*)/mutarjimiin
	mutarjima (*f.*)/mutarjimaat
trash, garbage	zibil, zbaala
travel	saafar/ysaafir (*rv*)
travel office	maktab safar
traveler's check	chakk siyaahi
treatment	⁹ilaaj
trench/s	khandaq/khanaadiq
trip/s	safra/safraat
good trip	*safra sa⁹iida*
trunk/s, box/s	sanduug/sanaadiig
TV	talfizyoon
TV station	mahattat talfizyoon

U

umbrella/s	shamsiyya/shamsiyyaat
uncle/s (maternal)	khaal/khwaal
uncle/s (paternal)	⁹amm/⁹maam
understand	fiham/yifham (*rv*)
unhealthy	muu sihhi
United Nations	Munazzamat il-Umam
	il-Muttahida
university/s	jaami⁹a/jaami⁹aat
until	hatta, lil

upon, on	⁹ala/⁹a-
urgent	musta⁹jal (*m.*)
	musta⁹jala (*f.*)
urine	bool
U.S. administration	il-Idaara l-Amriikiyya
U.S. aid	il-Musaa⁹adaat
	il-Amriikiyya

V

vegetables	khuzrawaat
very much	hwaaya, jaziilan
video/s	vidyo/vidyoowaat
view/s	manzar/manaazir
village/s	qarya/quraa
visa/s	viiza/viiyaz
visit/s	ziyaara/ziyaaraat
visit	zaar/yzuur (*hv*)
vitamins	viitaamiinaat

W

waiter/s	booy/booyaat
waiting	intizaar
waiting room	ghurfat intizaar
walk	misha/yimshi (*wv*)
walking	mishi
wallet/s	jizdaan/jazaadiin

want	raad/yriid (*hv*)
warm	daafi (*m.*)/daafyiin
	daafya (*f.*)/daafyaat
warning	tah dhiir, indhaar
warning shots	talqaat tah dhiir
wash	ghisal yighsil (*rv*)
watch/s	saa⁹a/saa⁹aat
watch shop	saa⁹aati, mahal saa⁹aat
water/s	mayy/miyaah
clear water	*mayy saafi*
cold water	*mayy baarid*
contaminated water	*mayy mulawwath*
drinking water	*mayy shurub*
hot water	*mayy haar*
muddy water	*mayy khaabut*
water purification plant	ma⁹mal tasfiyat miyaah
water supply	tajhiizaat miyaah
water tank	hooz miyaah
water truck	loori miyaah
we	ihna
weak	za⁹iif (*m.*)/z⁹aaf
	za⁹iifa (*f.*)/z⁹aaf
weapon/s	slaah/asliha
weather	manaakh
week/s	usbuu⁹/asaabii⁹
weight/s	wazin/awzaan
Welcome.	ahlan wa sahlan.
well	zein (*m.*)/zeiniin
	zeina (*f.*)/zeinaat

West	gharb
Western	gharbi (*m.*)/gharbiyyiin
	gharbiyya (*f.*)/gharbiyyaat
What?	shunu/sh-?
What time is it?	ibbeish is-saa⁹a?
What's happening?	shaku maaku?
When?	shwakit?
Where?	wein?
Where from?	immein?, mnein?
Which?	ay?, yaa?
white	abyaz (*m.*)/biiz
	beiza (*f.*)/biizaat
Who?	minu?
Whose?	maalman?, ilman?
Why?	leish?
Why not?	leish laa?
wife/s	zooja/zoojaat
will, shall	rah-/ha-
wind	riyaah
window/s	shubbaak/shabaabiik
wine	nabiidh
wing/s (hospital)	radha/radhaat
winter	ish-Shita
wire/s	silik/aslaak
with	wiyya/ma⁹a
with pleasure	⁹ala ⁹eini
	iddallal (*m.*)/iddallalu
	idallali (*f.*)/iddallalu
witness/s	shaahid/shuhuud

woman/s	mara/niswaan
word/s	kalima/kalimaat
work/s	shughul/ashghaal, ⁹amal/a⁹maal
worker/s	⁹aamil/⁹ummaal
world	⁹aalam
write	kitab/yiktib (*rv*)
writing/s	kitaaba/kitaabaat
cuneiform writing	*kitaaba mismaariyya*
wrong/s, mistake/s	ghalat/aghlaat

Y

yard/s	yaarda/yaardaat
year/s	sana/sniin
yellow	asfar (*m.*)/sufur
	safra (*f.*)/sufur
yesterday	il-baarha
yes	na⁹am, 'ii
yogurt	liban
you	inta (*m.*)/intu
	inti (*f.*)/intu

Z

ziggurat/s	zaqquura/zaqquuraat

About the Author

Dr. Yasin Alkalesi is a respected lecturer in the areas of Arab culture and archaeology of the Middle East. He is one of the country's top Arabic translators and the founder of ARABICO Inc. in Los Angeles. Since the 1980s, ARABICO has provided a variety of services to U.S. companies and organizations, including cross-cultural training programs, development of audiovisual materials, qualitative market research, and Arabic language instruction. His language programs cover Arab culture, customs, and business practices, and are designed for U.S. executives and managers working in the Arab world.

Dr. Alkalesi holds a Ph.D. in Near Eastern archaeology and languages from Yale University and bachelor's and master's degrees in archaeology and history from the University of Baghdad. He is a senior lecturer of Arabic and archaeology at the University of California, Los Angeles, and has taught Arabic at Yale and California State University, Fullerton. He is an active member of several educational and business associations concerned with American and Arab affairs.

Dr. Alkalesi has contributed many articles, monographs, and books in the fields of Middle East languages and archaeology. He is also the author of *Modern Iraqi Arabic: A Textbook*, published by Georgetown University Press (2001).